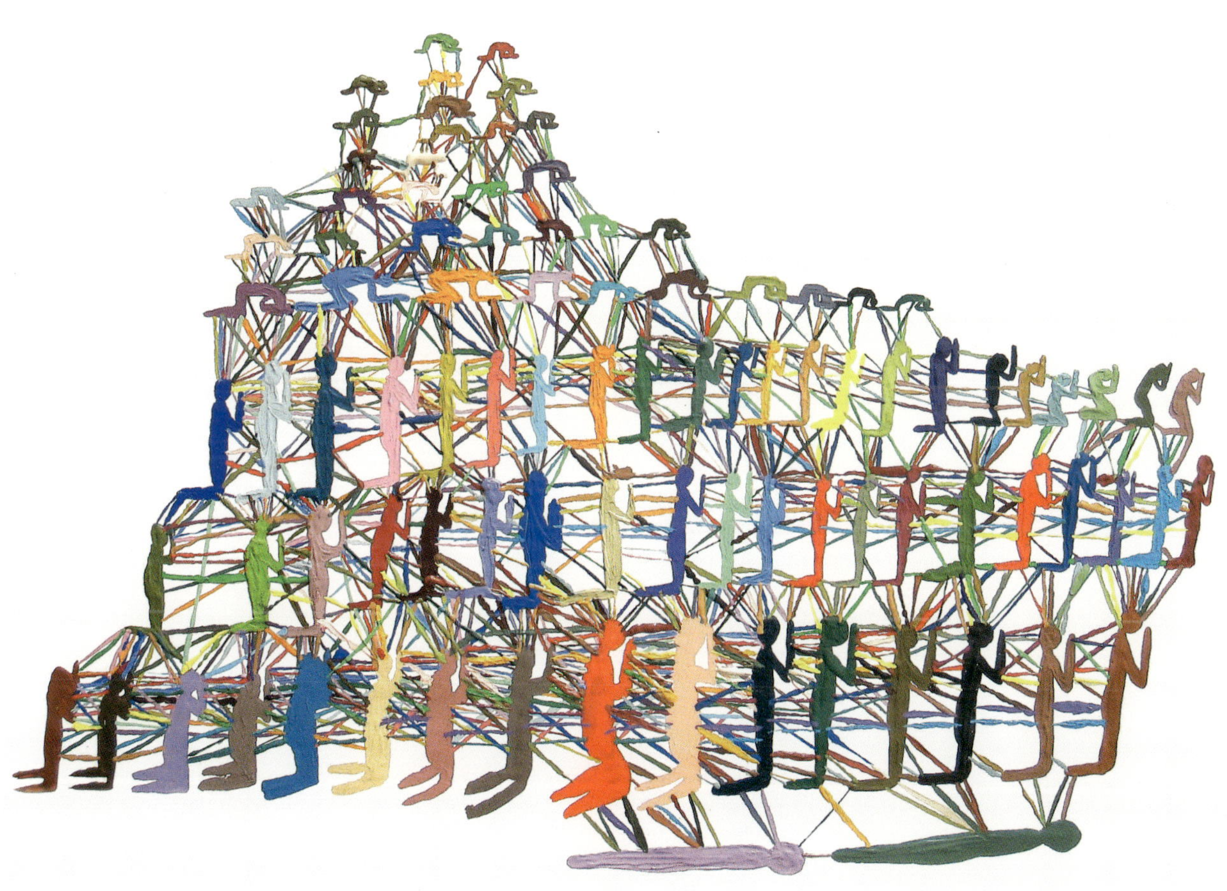

**TERRI LINDBLOOM**
CURATOR

**CRAIG ADCOCK**
ESSAY

**MUSEUM OF FINE ARTS**
October 12 - November 16, 2007

**FLORIDA STATE UNIVERSITY**
College of Visual Arts, Theatre & Dance

This program was organized by the Florida State University Museum of Fine Arts with grant assistance from the Florida Arts Council of the State of Florida, the University Arts & Humanities Program Enhancement Grant, and the Leon County Cultural Development Program. Educational Programming is supported through the State Partners Grant Initiative of the City of Tallahassee Cultural Services, Cultural Resources Commission.

## PROJECT SUPPORT AND ORGANIZATION

RUNNING AROUND THE POOL was organized by the Florida State University Museum of Fine Arts. Guest Curator: Terri Lindbloom. Essayist: Craig Adcock. Project Staff: Allys Palladino-Craig, Grantwriter and Editor; Stephanie Tessin, Exhibition Registrar; Michelle Newell, Editorial Assistant; Jean Young, Fiscal Officer; Teri Yoo, Communications Officer; Viki D. Thompson Wylder, Educational Programming; Wayne Vonada, Senior Preparator.

*This program is sponsored in part by:*

The State of Florida,

Department of State,

Division of Cultural Affairs,

Florida Arts Council, and the

National Endowment for the Arts.

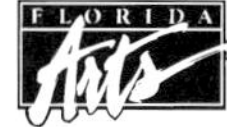

The City of Tallahassee State Partners Grant

Initiative and the

Leon County Cultural

Development Grant Program, both

administered by the

Council on Culture & Arts.

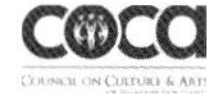

The publication was underwritten by an Arts & Humanities Program Enhancement Grant to Guest Curator Terri Lindbloom from the Council on Research and Creativity at Florida State University.

Design: Julienne T. Mason, JJKLM, Lansing, Michigan
Pre-press Graphics: Daniel McInnis, Progressive Printing
Printer: Progressive Printing, Jacksonville, Florida



Title Page: Chris Johanson, *Untitled (Praying People)*, acrylic on paper, 2006, 17.5 x 23.5 inches. Courtesy of the Artist and Kavi Gupta Gallery, New York.

## LENDERS TO THE EXHIBITION

Bank, Los Angeles

Cheim & Read Gallery, New York

Clementine Gallery, New York

CRG Gallery, New York

David Castillo Gallery, Miami

David Zwirner, New York

Deitch Projects, New York

Gallery Paule Anglim, San Francisco

Gavin Brown's enterprise, New York

Gregory Lind Gallery, San Francisco

Heather Marx Gallery, San Francisco

Kavi Gupta Gallery, Chicago

Kevin Bruk Gallery, Miami

Meridian Gallery, New York

Morgan Lehman Gallery, New York

1310PE, Los Angeles

PaceWildenstein, New York

Paul Morris Gallery, New York

Priska Juschka Fine Art, New York

SandroniRey, Los Angeles

Sean Kelly Gallery, New York

Shoshana Wayne Gallery, Santa Monica

The Project, New York

303 Gallery, New York

COLLECTIONS:

Matt Aberle

Christian Haye

Nedra and Mark Oren

Martina Yamin

Private Collections

## CURATOR'S NOTE

*The current resurgence of drawing in recent years, is perhaps the first moment in history when artists can opt for drawing as their principal medium, confident in the knowledge that their work will not suffer in status as a result.*
—Emma Dexter*

Drawing's historic roots are deep—from that first mysterious, primal mark on a cave wall to the preliminary sketch for something more expansive than itself to the current lure of drawing for the sake of drawing with un-restrained creativity. Within the past ten years, drawing has evolved into a stand-alone medium. This evolution and growth can be attributed in part to the shifting boundaries of installation, sculpture, and time-based media such as video, animation and performance art that have welcomed drawing into their arenas. In addition, the blending of craft and high art has also influenced drawing as seen in works that utilize cartooning and illustrative imagery as well as alternative materials like thread, wire, and chocolate syrup.

The artists in this exhibition were chosen for their remarkable freedom and diversity. *Running around the Pool* was created to allow viewers to experience a few of the after effects of these changes during this amazing period in the history of mark making. Some artists in the exhibition have chosen the format of installation, sculpture or street art while others take a more traditional approach with a flat two-dimensional surface utilizing watercolor, pencil and / or collage. A wide variety of genres is present in this exhibition including narrative, abstract, expressionistic, representational, cultural and political. These artists may have been influenced and inspired by the past but, as experienced in this exhibition, they push "the boundaries of drawing in fresh [alternative] directions"*—outside the perimeter of the historic pool.

Terri Lindbloom
Department of Art
Florida State University

---

*Both quotations from Emma Dexter, *Vitamin D, New Perspectives in Drawing* (London and New York: Phaidon Press, 2005), pages 8 and 5.

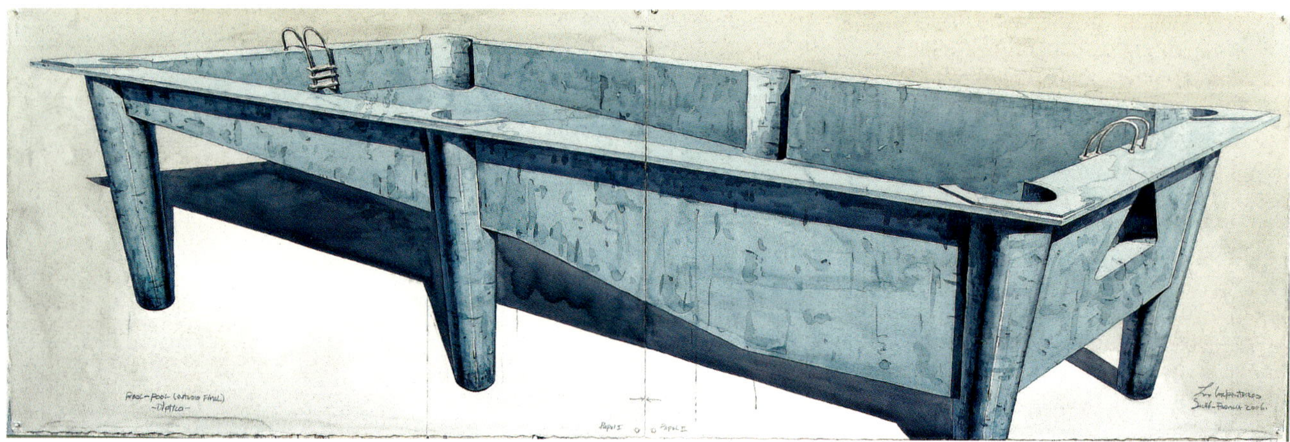

Los Carpinteros, *Pool-Pool (Estudio Final)*, 2006, watercolor on paper, diptych, 29 x 85 inches framed. Collection of Nedra and Mark Oren. Courtesy of Sean Kelly Gallery, New York.

Craig Adcock teaches modern and contemporary art history at the University of Iowa. His recent publications include essays about Marcel Duchamp, Arakawa, and James Rosenquist. He is currently working on a revision of his book about Duchamp.

The works in *Running around the Pool* can evoke images of both real and imagined worlds. They can conjure up vast cosmological reaches or bring to mind city streets falling to pieces. They can seem emotionally detached or politically engaged. They can confront difficult issues such as warfare, child abuse, racism, and being burned at the stake; or they can engage innocuous subject matters such as piles of rocks and barren landscapes. The drawings in the exhibition are multivalent and hybrid. The artists who produced them are versatile, and the artistic affinities they share are wide-ranging. Their influences come from cartoons, graphic and digital design, biology, astronomy, medieval embroidery, and graffiti—not to mention their art historical affiliations with Dada, Surrealism, Abstract Expressionism, Pop Art, California Funk, Chicago Imagism, Minimalism, and Conceptual Art. Some of the works in the exhibition look futuristic; others look old-fashioned. Some are small, intimate sketches; others are large, encompassing installations. Some are roughed in; others are highly finished. What they all share is a capacity to draw on deep sources of artistic wit and creative energy.

The meaning of the word "drawing" involves the notion of pulling something out, as in "drawing a card" or "drawing a gun." The most general sense of the term suggests arriving somewhere, as in "drawing a conclusion" or "drawing a distinction"—the use referred to here in the title.[1] In art and art history, drawing also implies the process of conceiving a work of art, of designing its constituent parts. As Francis Ames-Lewis has pointed out, this role has been fundamental to drawing at least since the early Renaissance: "During the fifteenth century conventional compositions and figure-types needed more and more to be reconsidered according to the new tenets of early Renaissance realism, so artists were stimulated to develop the scope of drawing which came to be seen as the natural medium for investigating new problems."[2] Then, artists used their drawings, as they do now, to form and to organize their works. What is perhaps different now is that drawing is no longer seen as a medium that is preliminary to making a painting or a sculpture, or to designing a building. Drawing is now fully accepted as an independent art form.[3] To be sure, the intellectual aspects of drawing are still basic to its practice. Drawing is now, as it has been for the last 500 years, in many ways equivalent to artistic thinking, and it continues "to be seen as the natural medium for investigating new problems." Through drawing, artists project their thoughts, their artistic conceptualizations, onto a surface or into a space.

As a way of pulling creative ideas out of wherever it is they come from, drawing is a discursive, critical practice. It can also be largely intuitive. It can range from being spontaneously sketchy to being painstakingly studied. Drawing underpins the work of art at the beginning and at the end of the creative process. It helps artists to capture their most preliminary impressions and to elaborate their most fully realized

---


1   After this essay was underway, I came across an exhibition catalogue with the title *Drawing Distinctions: American Drawings of the Seventies* by Alfred Kren (Munich: Prestel-Verlag, 1981). The catalogue has a Process Art orientation and includes drawings by Richard Artschwager, Jonathan Borofsky, Linda Francis, Robert Grosvenor, Will Insley, Barry Le Va, Bill Lundberg, Gordon Matta-Clark, Bruce Nauman, Stephen Rosenthal, Fred Sandback, Joel Shapiro, Paul Sharits, Keith Sonnier, Paul Thek, James Turrell, Richard Tuttle, William Wegman, and Robert Wilson. These artists can be thought of as representing an early stage of postmodern practice just as the artists in the present exhibition can be thought of as representing a late stage in postmodern practice. Susan L. Feagin, from a somewhat more traditional perspective than I am adopting here, has discussed how we can draw "distinctions" between different kinds of drawing; see her "Pictorial Representation and the Act of Drawing," *American Philosophical Quarterly* 24 (1987): 161-70. Also useful is Feagin's article in the *Encyclopedia of Aesthetics*, s.v. "Drawing." Among the best recent studies is Michael Newman, "The Marks, Traces, and Gestures of Drawing," in *The Stage of Drawing: Gesture and Act*, exh. cat. (London: Tate Publishing; New York: Drawing Center, 2003), 93-108.

2   Francis Ames-Lewis, *Drawing in Early Renaissance Italy*, rev. ed. (New Haven and London: Yale University Press, 2000), 17.

3   Bernice Rose makes this point in her survey of late-modern drawing, *Drawing Now*, exh. cat. (New York: Museum of Modern Art, 1976), 9; see also her chapter, "A View of Drawing Today," in *Drawing: History of an Art*, by Geneviève Monnier (Geneva: Skira; New York: Rizzoli, 1979), 200-252. The centrality of drawing in contemporary art has been noted by Emma Dexter; see her "Introduction," in *Vitamin D: New Perspectives in Drawing* (London and New York: Phaidon Press, 2005), 8: "While most artists since the Renaissance practiced, prized, and acknowledged the special qualities of drawing in contradistinction to those of painting and sculpture, the current resurgence of drawing in recent years is perhaps the first moment in history when artists can opt for drawing as their principal medium, confident in the knowledge that their work will not suffer in status as a result."

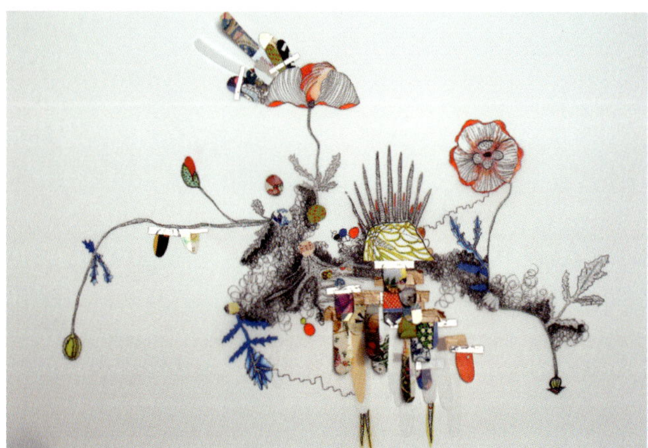

Janae Easton, *The Growth of a Poppy*, 2007, Mylar, Lenox 100, wrapping paper, colored marker, colored pencil, pen, foil tape, duct tape, and other found papers, 25 x 40 inches.

visualizations. Through drawing, artists decide what to say and how to say it. They use their drawing as their basic language, and from this perspective, they use lines much like writers use words.[4] In the process of drafting a text, words are drawn from a general matrix of thought, just as, in the process of composing a drawing, lines are pulled from a background of what might be called sightings—sightings that can be mere glimpses or prolonged inspections. Both drawing and writing help artists, and authors, to see more clearly, although just how either procedure actually works remains a mystery.

There has, of course, been a great deal of philosophical discussion about the correlations that exist between words and images. In terms of writing, Maurice Merleau-Ponty, for example, once argued, following Ferdinand de Saussure, that meaning lies in the spaces between words, that it depends on grammatical relationships.[5] In his comparison of painting and language, Merleau-Ponty suggested that it is not possible to give priority of meaning to one over the other.[6] In the drawings brought together by Terri Lindbloom for *Running around the Pool*, an equivalency often exists between visual and linguistic elements. In these drawings, too, it is difficult to give more weight to the images than to the words. The issues at stake in the comparison have been addressed by Jean-François Lyotard. In his discussion of what he calls the "differend," he suggests that

relationship problems separate linguistic phrases. He argues, following Ludwig Wittgenstein, that inevitable heterogeneities lie between different human "language games":

> A phrase, even the most ordinary one, is constituted according to a set of rules (its regimen). There are a number of phrase regimens: reasoning, knowing, describing, recounting, questioning, showing, ordering, etc. Phrases from heterogeneous regimens cannot be translated from one into the other. They can be linked one onto the other in accordance with an end fixed by a genre of discourse.[7]

The genre of discourse at work in contemporary drawing is complex, involving all these regimes: reasoning, knowing, describing, recounting, questioning, showing, ordering, etc. And it finds there all kinds of unexpected—and untranslatable—linkages.

Most of the drawings in *Running around the Pool* are, in one way or another, "representational," even though, in these late-postmodern times, or perhaps better, these (post-)postmodern times, the term is problematic. Indeed, in the context of the show, it is not completely clear how the word "representational" should be taken. Robert Storr, in a recent general study entitled *Modern Art "despite" Modernism*, brackets his discussion with two groups of drawings, which he refers to as "drawing lessons."[8] What he thinks we should learn is that the contents of "modernism" are larger than generally assumed. The book is about the history of representational art in the twentieth century and traces the alternative tradition that parallels modernist abstraction. As one might expect, the majority of the drawings—by such artists as John D. Graham, Lucian Freud, David Hockney, and Antonio López García—are realistic portraits, figure studies, and still-life compositions. They depict recognizable people and objects. The works in *Running around the Pool* rarely conform to this model, and they seldom fit into the category of "alternative modernist art," even though they too depict recognizable people and objects. The majority of the drawings are not modern; they are not even postmodern.

Among the most obvious characteristics of the drawings in *Running around the Pool* is their mixed media nature. They use means ranging from graphite, colored pencil, charcoal and pastel, to oil stick, aerosol spray paint, watercolor, gouache, ink, acrylic, thread, wire, and monofilament. They use a variety of collage elements including found objects, found works of art, pieces of cardboard, and quilted fabric.

4    For a discussion of the parallels, from the point of view of psychoanalysis, see Serge Tisseron, "All Writing Is Drawing: The Spatial Development of the Manuscript," in *Boundaries: Writing and Drawing* , ed. Martine Reid, Yale French Studies, no. 84 (New Haven, Conn.: Yale University Press, 1994), 29-42. This essay was brought to my attention by Catherine de Zegher, "The Stage of Drawing," in *The Stage of Drawing: Gesture and Act*, exh. cat. (London: Tate Publishing; New York: Drawing Center, 2003), 267-78; de Zegher's discussion is also useful in the present context.

5    Maurice Merleau-Ponty, "Eye and Mind," trans. Michael B. Smith, in *The Merleau-Ponty Aesthetics Reader: Philosophy and Painting*, ed. Galen A. Johnson and Michael B. Smith (Evanston, Ill.: Northwestern University Press, 1993), 121-49. Saussure's diacritical explanation of language is put into context by Mieke Bal and Norman Bryson, "Semiotics and Art History," *Art Bulletin* 73 (1991): 174-208; also useful is their article in the *Encyclopedia of Aesthetics*, s.v. "Semiotics: Semiotics as a Theory of Art."

6    See Gary Shapiro, *Encyclopedia of Aesthetics*, s.v. "French Aesthetics."

7    Jean-François Lyotard, *The Differend: Phrases in Dispute*, trans. Georges Van Den Abbeele (Minneapolis: University of Minnesota Press, 1988), xii. For Wittgenstein on "language games," see his *Philosophical Investigations*, 3rd ed., trans. G. E. M. Anscombe (Oxford: Blackwell, 2001); for an analysis of the concept, see G. P. Baker and P. M. S. Hacker, *Wittgenstein: Understanding and Meaning*, vol. 1 of *An Analytical Commentary on the "Philosophical Investigations"* (Chicago: University of Chicago Press, 1980), 89-98.

8    Robert Storr, *Modern Art "despite" Modernism* (New York: Museum of Modern Art; distributed by Abrams, 2000), 2-15, 232-43.

Among the technical processes used are hot glue on Plexiglas, oil paint and acrylic on Mylar, paper silhouette assemblage, and photo reproductions on three-dimensional forms.

In trying to describe the kind of representationalism being used by many of these artists, expressions like "can't quite make out what's going on" or "can't quite determine the imagery" come to mind, or at least they come to this writer's mind. Janae Easton's drawings, for example, are among the most abstract in the exhibition. Her compositions, including *Growth of a Poppy* and *Robust Bark Encountered by Dusky Caves*, which are part of *Running around the Pool*, suggest flower and plant forms without resolving into recognizable images of specific natural objects. They represent, in a more general way, the categories of growth and decomposition.[9] What might be called her "abstract representationalism," like so much of the work in the exhibition, uses an exuberant form of address. Indeed, her works can come right off the wall to invade the three-dimensional space of the gallery. Rosalind Krauss has associated such lines of attack with Georges Bataille and a heterological "art of excess." She traces this impulse to Jean Dubuffet with his interests in dealing with raw matter such as dirt and offal.[10] Dubuffet and art brut do suggest themselves as possible sources, not just for Easton, but for many of the artists in the exhibition.

By disregarding the conventions of both abstraction and representation, the artists in *Running around the Pool* produce works that cannot comfortably be co-opted into the traditions of Modernism, even the alternative Modernism outlined by Storr. To be sure, they operate against the general cultural background of Modernism, but they do so using it as a foil. For Bataille, Édouard Manet had broken "rhetoric's grip on painting, as a silencing of speech in order to discover the preeminence of vision as such."[11] Art is now once again connected to speech, and the more heterological its approaches become, the more it obliges us to recognize its fundamentally uncommon relationship to bodily experience. There is no modernist "vision as such." There is rather, as Bataille goes on to suggest, an embodied sense of sight that avers the content of vision, irrespective of how that content is represented in a work of art.[12] Jackson Pollock once said that he didn't like the term "abstract expressionism," and that he didn't think either "non-objective" or "non-representational" accurately described his painting: "I'm very representational some of the time, and a little all of the time."[13]

An unconventional representationalism is also characteristic of Russell Crotty's art. His detailed ink drawings initially appear to be quite abstract. In some cases, they are applied to Lucite or fiberglass spheres suspended inside gallery spaces. These geometrical forms may at first seem to be minimalist sculptures, but their subtle visual textures invite closer inspection. Crotty's drawings are influenced by his activities as an amateur

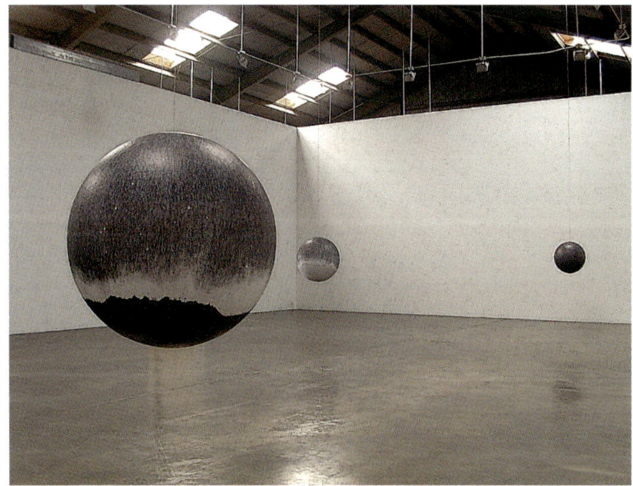

Russell Crotty, installation view from his exhibition in 2000 at Shoshana Wayne Gallery in Santa Monica, California. Photograph courtesy of Shoshana Wayne Gallery.

astronomer, and they illustrate the night sky seen from his observatory. They sometimes show the surrounding horizon, as can be seen in *Vineyard Potential*, the work included in *Running around the Pool*. Viewers have a sense that they are looking at the celestial vault of heaven from the outside in. Crotty also writes diaristic observations around the edges of his drawings expatiating on such matters as the effects of light pollution and urban sprawl. These notations give his works an ecological overtone.[14] The macrocosm-in-microcosm forms that Crotty uses are comparable to the cut-paper works of Chris Natrop.[15] Natrop's large template-like patterns, which at first seem quite abstract, are also suspended by monofilament inside gallery spaces. Their silhouettes, together with the shadows they cast onto wall surfaces, suggest the shapes one might glimpse while moving through a forest or a lush flower garden. They provide the viewer with an ambiguous shadow puppet show that constantly draws and redraws itself as the forms move back and forth. The cut paper imagery, which hints at plants being harvested and processed, gives his works, like those of Crotty, an environmental nuance.

Wendy Wischer's drawings are diverse and can range from images created by burning paper with sunlight focused by magnifying lenses, as seen in *Sunspot Diaries*, to plastic cases filled with piles of small paper cutouts, as seen in *Longing*. Works such as these are grounded in a vocabulary of technical practice geared toward revealing the hidden content of what might seem inconsequential and commonplace. Wischer

9    Janae Easton, http://www.re-title.com/artists/Janae-Easton.asp.

10   Rosalind Krauss, "Antivision," *October*, no. 36 (Spring 1986): 147-54.

11   Ibid., 153.

12   Ibid.

13   Jackson Pollock (1956) in Selden Rodman, *Conversations with Artists* (New York: Devin-Adair, 1957), 82; reprinted in *Jackson Pollock: A Catalogue Raisonné of Paintings, Drawings and Other Works*, ed. Francis V. O'Connor and Eugene V. Thaw, vol. 4 (New Haven, Conn., and London: Yale University Press, 1978), 275.

14   This point is made by Martin Herbert, "Russell Crotty," in *Vitamin D: New Perspectives in Drawing* (London and New York: Phaidon Press, 2005), 66; see also Michael Wilson, "Russell Crotty," *Artforum International* 41 (December 2002): 138-39; and Laura Hoptman, "Science and Art, Nature and Artifice," *Drawing Now: Eight Propositions*, exh. cat. (New York: Museum of Modern Art, 2002), 16.

15   Chris Natrop, http://www.chrisnatrop.com.

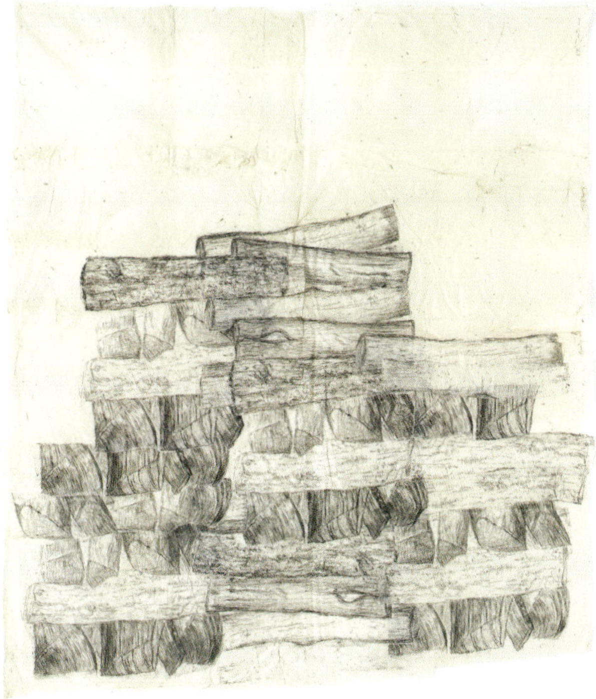

Kiki Smith, *Pyre*, 2001, ink on Nepal paper, 77.5 x 70 inches. Courtesy of the Artist and PaceWildenstein, New York.

says that she tries to find connections between dissimilar categories, especially between "natural" things and "artificial" things, and that by looking into "in-between" spaces, she can discover elusive entities and make them concrete.[16] Pae White's works are also diverse and can range from ethereal white and silver networks drawn on paper with spider web to sheets of Plexiglas laid on the floor of a gallery that cast undulating reflections onto the ceiling and surrounding walls. The artist is concerned with perceptual frameworks and with how they affect visual experience. By using unconventional, "non-art" materials—a kind of cross between Pop art and Light and Space installation—White creates striking visual effects in her works.[17] As one critic has expressed it, "the delighted responses they so effectively coax from the public are largely attributable to a perceived discrepancy between the modesty of their materials and execution and the near-sublime luxuriance of the outcome."[18] White's works often create spatial (and ideational) deformations between objects.

In the collage included in the current exhibition, *Noisy Letters (Blue), Noisy Letters (Green), Noisy Letters (Yellow)*, she basically camouflages the letter forms of the words "Blue," "Green," and "Yellow." The signal to noise ratio is such that the information in the Jasper Johns-like message is almost impossible to read.

In their drawings, Wischer and White manifest a kind of minimalist aesthetic, although neither artist is really involved with the conditions of minimalism. The artists are not aiming to eliminate illusionism in favor of abstraction, and they are not trying to abolish transcendence in favor of literalism. They are, more than anything else, interested in establishing continuities between such categories. Both Wischer and White use unusual techniques and shifting aesthetic categories to create works with more or less discernable content. Their works, like those of Crotty and Natrop, appear to be abstract at first glance. But on closer inspection, they turn out to be representational. Such works raise questions about what constitutes an "abstraction" or a "representation," and they bring to mind one of Ludwig Wittgenstein's famous statements:

> A main source of our failure to understand is that we do not *command* a *clear view* of the use of our words.—Our grammar is lacking in this sort of perspicuity. A perspicuous representation produces just that understanding which consists in "seeing connections." Hence the importance of finding and inventing *intermediate cases*.[19]

None of the artists under discussion here produce works that are exactly still-lifes or landscapes, nor do they create works that are precisely reductive sublimations. Rather, they find various kinds of "intermediate cases" that help us to see connections. Their drawings are both synoptic and non-specific, both concrete and abstract. Easton, for example, says that her "process connects with the ambiguity of the organic world, but is also inspired by Surrealism, landscape painting, assemblage, storytelling, how-to books, flower arranging, graffiti, cake decorating, flea markets, art brut, and the idea of slowness."[20] And Crotty suggests that his works, although they index the sublime in the sense of trying to express the inexpressible, also come down to earth: "Looking at a supernova remnant in Cygnus in the summer—it's like a very faint veil of gas. I can't put it in words, but I can attempt to draw it. It's almost a feeling. The really old light, this faint object, something cataclysmic we can't even imagine that happened 40,000 years ago is just drifting through the galaxy, and it happens to look really beautiful." Explaining how he uses his equipment, he says "I open the roof, pull the truck up, drop the tailgate, have coffee, snacks, and people just come over and hang out. . . . It's all about movement, time, and location. Location on a massive scale and location on an intimate scale."[21]

---


16    Wendy Wischer, http://www.wendywischer.com.

17    For a discussion of what's at stake in such work, see the following analysis of a group exhibition that included a piece by White: Dave Hickey, "The Murmur of Eloquence: Intimations of the Full World," in *Plane/Structures*, exh. cat., curated by David Pagel (Los Angeles: Otis Gallery, Otis College of Art and Design, 1994), 22-31; Joe Scanlan's essay, "Motivation and Time in the Work of Certain Los Angeles Artists," in ibid., 32-39, is also relevant. His comments about White are on p. 39.

18    Jan Tumlir, "Pae White," *Artforum International* 42 (Summer 2004): 255.

19    Wittgenstein, *Philosophical Investigations* (cited n. 7), sec. 122 (his emphasis).

20    Easton, unpublished artist's statement (provided by Florida State University).

21    Eileen Myles, "A Thousand Words: Russell Crotty Talks about His Atlases," *Artforum International* 40 (September 2001): 181.

Julie Mehretu is one of the most complex artists in *Running around the Pool*. Her work can also be described as "abstract representationalism." For the historian, the title of a recent exhibition catalogue of her work, *Julie Mehretu: Drawing into Painting*, recalls a similarly entitled catalogue, *Jackson Pollock: Drawing into Painting*.[22] Her swirling forms do suggest Pollock's paintings, and, especially from a distance, they seem to dissolve into abstract shapes. But they are also related to the virtual worlds of dystopian science fiction.[23] Made up of myriad fragments, ranging from architectural elements to abstract lines of force, her surfaces suggest birth and death, expansion and contraction, explosion and implosion, and they reference data immersion, visionics, cyberspace, and hyper-reality.[24] Like Pollock's drawings, her works seem to evolve spontaneously. Mehretu herself has commented on the gestural quality of her work:

> There is a definite visual similarity between my brushwork and Chinese calligraphy, as well as a conceptual similarity in the sense that in Chinese calligraphy every mark has a meaning and there is an energy that leads you where you are trying to get to: there is a way to paint the leaves on a tree, the grass on a hill or even the cosmos. In a way, I'm doing that in a more abstract way. When I started my investigation I wasn't necessarily being informed by Chinese calligraphy but now there is a conversation between the kind of mark making that I'm playing with and the kind you can see in Chinese calligraphy paintings, whether they are older or newer. There's a desire to describe the cosmos in a certain way, with marks that are indicators toward the cosmos as a system. I'm also using Japanese inks. The cosmology that the Surrealists were working with also informed my work.[25]

In a discussion of Cy Twombly, an artist whose works could also be compared with Mehretu's, Roland Barthes makes reference to the Japanese concept of *ma*, applying it to the often sparsely populated canvases of the abstract painter and draftsman.[26] Barthes suggests that the Japanese term is equivalent to the Latin word *rarus*, which can be translated as "rare." But the word also means "thin" or "far apart." The disparate elements in Mehretu's works, her abstract fragments and partial images, not only suggest divisions between various regimes, but also the rifts that can exist between diverse artistic arenas. In her exiguous, multi-layered surfaces,

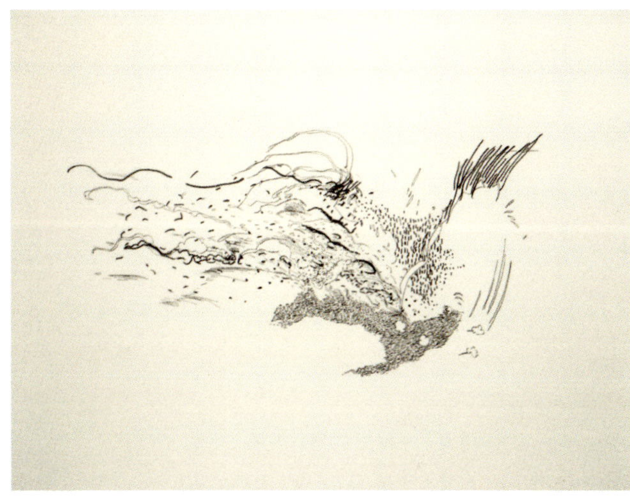

Julie Mehretu, *Untitled*, 2001, ink on mylar and paper, 19 x 20 inches. Collection of Christian Haye. Courtesy of The Project, New York.

the scrolls of Eastern art, occasionally interrupted by a gesture of flung ink, can be perceived.[27] And in addition to these rarefied spaces, the empty expanses of western art are apparent—not only those of Surrealism, which Mehretu alludes to, but also those of Abstract Expressionism. When looking at her works, both Roberto Matta and Jackson Pollock come to mind.[28] Merleau-Ponty characterized such thin and far-apart forms as being subject to radical change and transformation, indeed to metamorphosis: "Essence and existence, imaginary and real, visible and invisible—painting scrambles all our categories, spreading out before us its oneiric universe of carnal essences, actualized resemblances, mute meanings."[29]

The actualized resemblances and mute meanings of the drawings included in *Running around the Pool* create various kinds of oneiric universes. And despite our not being able to tell precisely what they represent, we are nevertheless perfectly right to ask what they stand for and what they signify. None of the works in the exhibition stands wholly against or outside iconographical meaning. They are never autonomous aesthetic objects in the modernist sense. The drawings of the artists discussed earlier—Easton, White, Wischer, Crotty, Natrop, and Mehretu—for

---

22 Douglas Fogle and Olukemi Ilesanmi, *Julie Mehretu: Drawing into Painting*, exh. cat. (Minneapolis: Walker Art Center, 2003); Bernice Rose, *Jackson Pollock: Drawing into Painting*, exh. cat. (New York: Museum of Modern Art, 1980).

23 The classic source here is probably William Gibson's *Neuromancer* (New York: Ace Books, 1984).

24 See Caroline A. Jones, "Fields of Intuition (in Four Proportions and Five Mods)," in *Remote Viewing (Invented Worlds in Recent Painting and Drawing)*, exh. cat., ed. Elisabeth Sussman (New York: Whitney Museum of American Art; distributed by Abrams, 2005), 81-95; also Hoptman, "Drafting an Architecture," *Drawing Now* (cited n. 14), 48.

25 Mehretu in an interview with Agustín Pérez Rubio, "Tracing the Universe of Julie Mehretu: A Choral Text," in *Julie Mehretu*, exh. cat. (León, Spain: MUSAC, Museo de Arte Contemporáneo de Castilla y León; Ostfildern, Germany: Hatje Cantz Verlag, 2007), 36.

26 Roland Barthes, "The Wisdom of Art," trans. Annette Lavers, in *Calligram: Essays in New Art History from France*, ed. Norman Bryson (Cambridge and New York: Cambridge University Press, 1988), 166-80, the quote is from p. 173.

27 For a discussion of the Japanese tradition of flung ink painting in relation to the gaze, see Norman Bryson, "The Gaze in the Expanded Field," in *Vision and Visuality*, ed. Hal Foster (Seattle, Wash.: Bay Press, 1988), 87-108.

28 See, for example, Faye Hirsch, "Full-Throttle Abstract," *Art in America* 92 (June - July 2004): 170.

29 Maurice Merleau-Ponty, "Eye and Mind," trans. Michael B. Smith, in *The Merleau-Ponty Aesthetics Reader: Philosophy and Painting*, ed. Galen A. Johnson and Michael B. Smith (Evanston, Ill.: Northwestern University Press, 1993), 121-49, the quote is from p. 130.

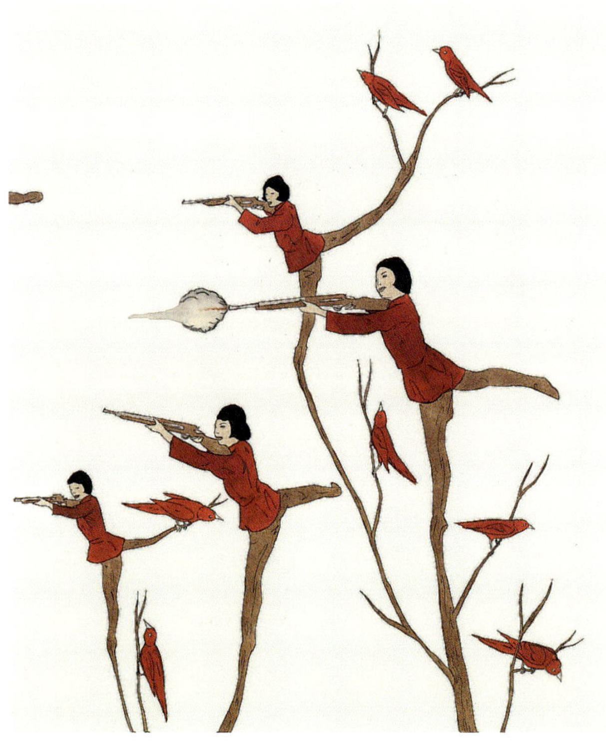

Marcel Dzama, Detail of *Eight Strong Winds*, 2005, ink and watercolor on paper, 4-part drawing, each drawing 14 x 11 inches, 28 x 22 inches overall. Private Collection, New York. Courtesy of David Zwirner, New York.

in part, what makes the art worthwhile, and its involvedness is, in part, what makes it enjoyable. The drawings do not demand an expert physical capability on the part of the artists alone; they also require a mental adroitness on our part and insist that we work together with the artists. Drawing then is not only a form of art, but also a form of participation. We trace relationships. We act in concert with the artists, building up those dreamy worlds suggested by Merleau-Ponty.

There is not only an oneiric, but also an aleatory quality to the way these processes work together. Much depends on what we bring to specific drawings as specific viewers. We can play language games, both linguistic and visual, in more or less random ways. And all kinds of inadvertencies can transpire as we shape outlines, draw connections, and align configurations, and map colors onto their appropriate areas. Chance can also figure in the way the artists themselves work. Raymond Pettibon has pointed out that accidents often influence the final outcome of his drawings. He says that he welcomes such chance interventions. He also points out that contingency is basic to the way he composes his texts. The drawing in the current exhibition shows a baseball player at bat. On it are several handwritten statements: "It was fine to watch him do it." "Yes, I must give my readers that." "17." "88." ".303." How we interpret the drawing in view of these words and numbers depends on many things, including our recollections of how we played the game, or didn't, our knowledge of the rules of the game, and our views of professional sports, in general.

Pettibon says that when he writes such statements on his drawings, although he may start out with a plan or an idea, he can wind up saying something completely unexpected: "there is also writing that is more open, more associational, and even accidental. You don't necessarily know where it's going to go while you're doing it."[31] For writers, the act of writing calls forth ideas just as often as ideas call forth writing. And for artists, the act of drawing, as Pettibon suggests, generates concepts just as often as concepts generate drawing. Some designs are anticipated and planned, others seem to appear on the page without any conscious input from the artist. Kiki Smith has also emphasized this "unbidden" aspect of art making: "I think art is just a way to have an opportunity to think about things. I don't have any place that I'm trying to make it go. I'm not trying to control it at all. It's like standing in the wind and letting it pull you where, whatever direction, it wants you to go . . . and things start telling you what you're supposed to pay attention to. It really just comes in you and tells you, 'Pay attention to this and make this.' I have lots of things where my work just said, 'Make it like this.'"[32]

Among the striking works that Smith has recently produced is a sculptural group of women being immolated. *Woman on Pyre* and *Pyre*, the drawings included in the current exhibition, are related to this work. At one level, the images are about innocence, since no woman ever placed on a pyre was guilty of being a witch or deserved to be burned alive. Smith is adept at handling such extreme situations. She is famous

example, refer, at the very least, to structural and organizational themes, even though we may initially misconstrue what they say or fail to recognize what they represent. Through the act of questioning them, we may discover their greatest appeal, even though that process may also preclude our ever finding any universal key to their meaning.

Whatever the case may be, such scrutiny is interesting. As Jean-Paul Sartre argued, the act of looking, in a sense, determines the status of the viewer in the presence of what is being looked at. George Bauer has reminded us that, for Sartre, the work of art "does not belong to the real world but appears when the real world is negated by 'the intentional act of an imagining consciousness.' The aesthetic object is not part of the world of experience but is grasped through the act of the viewer."[30] The drawings in *Running around the Pool* are comprehended in just such intellectual terms. They encourage us to seek clarification about matters that are not easily discerned, that are not easily surveyed. Our having this difficulty is,

---

30    George H. Bauer, *Sartre and the Artist* (Chicago and London: University of Chicago Press, 1969), 3; Sartre's discussion, from which the quote is taken, occurs in the conclusion of his *L'Imaginaire: Psychologie phénoménologique de l'imagination* (Paris: Gallimard, 1940), 239.

31    Raymond Pettibon in *Art 21: Art in the Twenty-First Century*, vol. 2 (New York: Abrams, 2001), 159.

32    Kiki Smith in *Art 21: Art in the Twenty-First Century*, vol. 2 (New York: Abrams, 2001), 38.

for her works that deal with the vicissitudes of individual existence, particularly the physical suffering that flesh is heir to. Many of her works use the human body and its constituent parts and fluids—internal organs, flayed muscles, blood, semen, urine—to examine mortality. The artist also responds to social forces related to such issues—the politics of abortion and the AIDS crisis, for example.[33] By depicting men and women in various extreme states—rapture, torture, abjection—Smith unpacks common experiences that are rarely examined in art. She also portrays less common events—resurrection, transmigration, transmogrification—and these too allow her to address matters that are indescribable, even unspeakable. Smith sometimes conjoins human beings with animals, and more rarely with plants, and the creatures born from such unions are disquieting, if not monstrous. The hybrid bodies—human, animal, vegetal—become conduits for joy and despair, vessels that are both sacred and profane. Smith may not have intended the mythological overtones in her works, but they are nevertheless there for us to interpret: "I don't really like a tight narrative," she says. "I'm too jumpy or something. I don't want to be so declarative. I'd rather make something that's very open-ended that then can have a meaning to me, but then somebody else can fill it up with meaning."[34]

Like Smith's works, the drawings in *Running around the Pool* can be read using shifting terms. Their fluctuant referents open them to being filled in various ways and to various levels. In many cases, the drawings are composed using both words and images. In a sense, they are about the open-ended nature of words and images. The drawings, polysemic in several senses of the term, bring with them the traditions of western art history, a history that now includes the most diverse postmodern responses. Many, perhaps most, of the drawings foreground the fact that they began as blank pages, as mere potentialities, or perhaps better, as mere portents.[35] In this regard, of course, they began life much like the blank sheets encountered by Leonardo da Vinci, Nicolas Poussin, Paul Cézanne, Marcel Duchamp, Jackson Pollock, Richard Serra, and Sigmar Polke. In the context of a more sprawling contemporary visual culture, the drawings in *Running around the Pool* reject the optimism associated with Modernism. They reject that earlier moment's confidence in the future and, instead, project traits that can never remain fixed.[36] These drawings always require completion. They take on their characters, ones that are both actual and conceptual, as we read and decipher them. Our interactions with them serve to point up the infinitely complex separations (inadequacies) that lie between descriptive surfaces and narrative depths.[37]

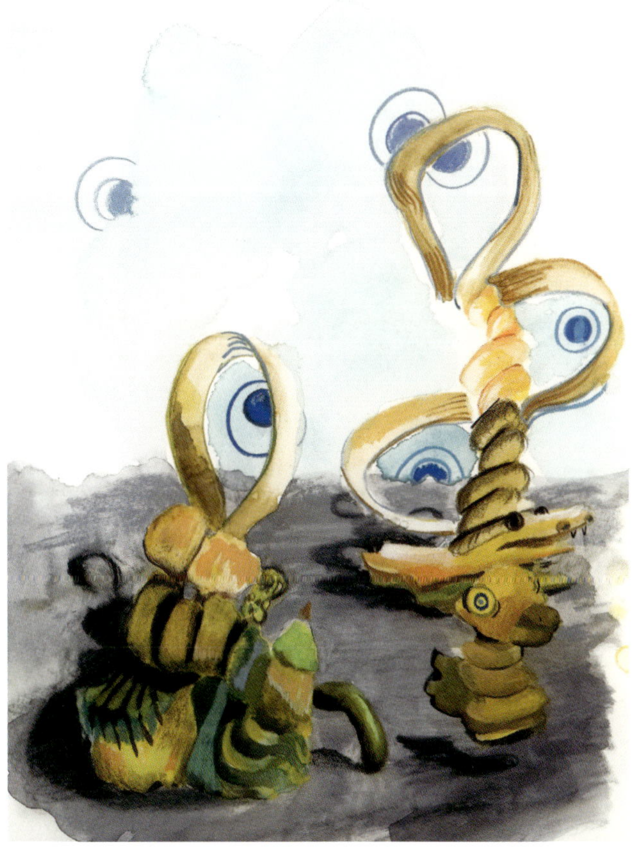

Laura Owens, *Untitled*, 2005, watercolor, pencil, pastel on paper 14 x 10 1/4 inches. Collection of Martina Yamin. Courtesy of the Artist and Gavin Brown's enterprise, New York.

As has been suggested, contemporary drawings are generally representational. But they are also presentational. They present things directly. Most of the artists in the current exhibition take on, and take from,

33    Helaine Posner, "Approaching Grace," *Kiki Smith* (New York: Monacelli Press, 2005), 7-35; see also Linda Nochlin, "Unholy Postures: Kiki Smith and the Body," in *Kiki Smith: A Gathering, 1980-2005*, exh. cat., ed. Siri Engberg (Minneapolis, Minn.: Walker Art Center, 2005), 30-37. For an appraisal that puts Smith's work in perspective, see Christine Ross, "Redefinitions of Abjection in Contemporary Performances of the Female Body," *Res*, no. 31 (Spring 1997): 149-56.

34    Smith in *Art 21: Art in the Twenty-First Century*, vol. 2 (New York: Abrams, 2001), 46.

35    For a discussion germane to these points, see Norman Bryson, "A Walk for a Walk's Sake," in *The Stage of Drawing: Gesture and Act*, exh. cat. (London: Tate Publishing; New York: Drawing Center, 2003), 149-58. I have also dealt with these issues in an earlier essay; see Craig Adcock, "The Meaning of Blank in Arakawa's Early Work," *Interfaces: Image/Texte/Language*, no. 21/22 (2004): 203-15.

36    In French, the term "trait" can, of course, mean both a "trace" and a drawn "line." Jacques Derrida discusses the word in the first part of *Memoirs of the Blind: The Self-Portrait and Other Ruins*, trans. Pascale-Anne Brault and Michael Naas (Chicago and London: University of Chicago Press, 1993); for another interesting analysis, see Hubert Damisch, *Traité du trait* (Paris: Réunion des Musées Nationaux, 1995).

37    E. H. Gombrich called this half of the interchange the "Beholder's Share," part 3 of *Art and Illusion: A Study in the Psychology of Pictorial Representation* (London: Phaidon Press, 1960), 154-244; for another traditional discussion, see Richard Wollheim, "On Drawing an Object," *On Art and the Mind: Essays and Lectures* (London: Allen Lane, 1973), 3-30. For two of the best, and deepest, contributions to interpretation theory, see Hans-Georg Gadamer, *Truth and Method*, 2nd rev. ed., translation revised by Joel Weinsheimer and Donald G. Marshall (New York: Crossroad, 1989); and Paul Ricoeur, *The Rule of Metaphor: The Creation of Meaning in Language*, trans. Robert Czerny, Kathleen McLaughlin, and John Costello (London: Routledge, 2003).

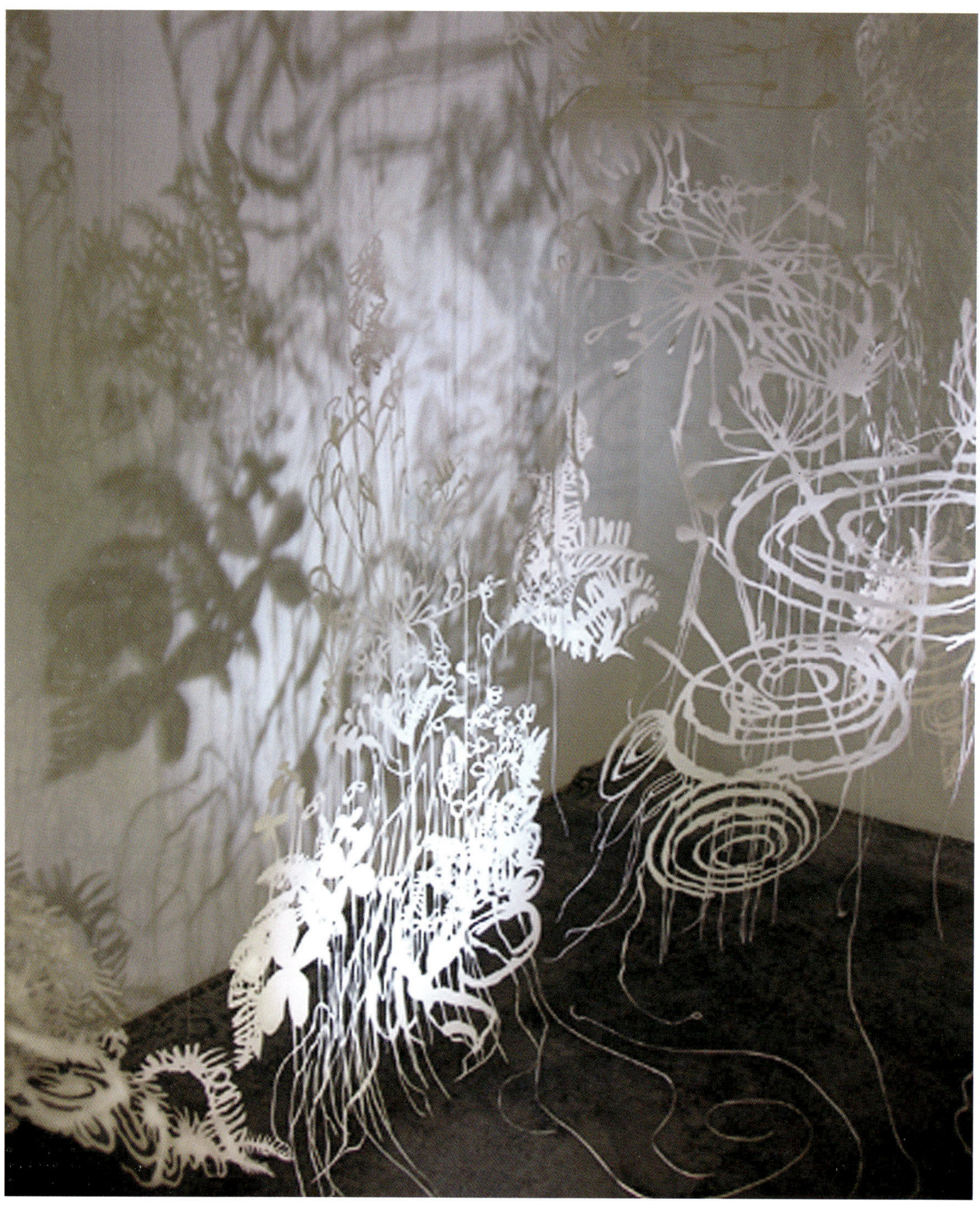

Chris Natrop, Detail from *Fern Space Burst*, 2004, hand cut paper, colored ink, watercolor, irridescent medium, tape, thread, 10 x 8 x 8 feet. Courtesy of the Artist.

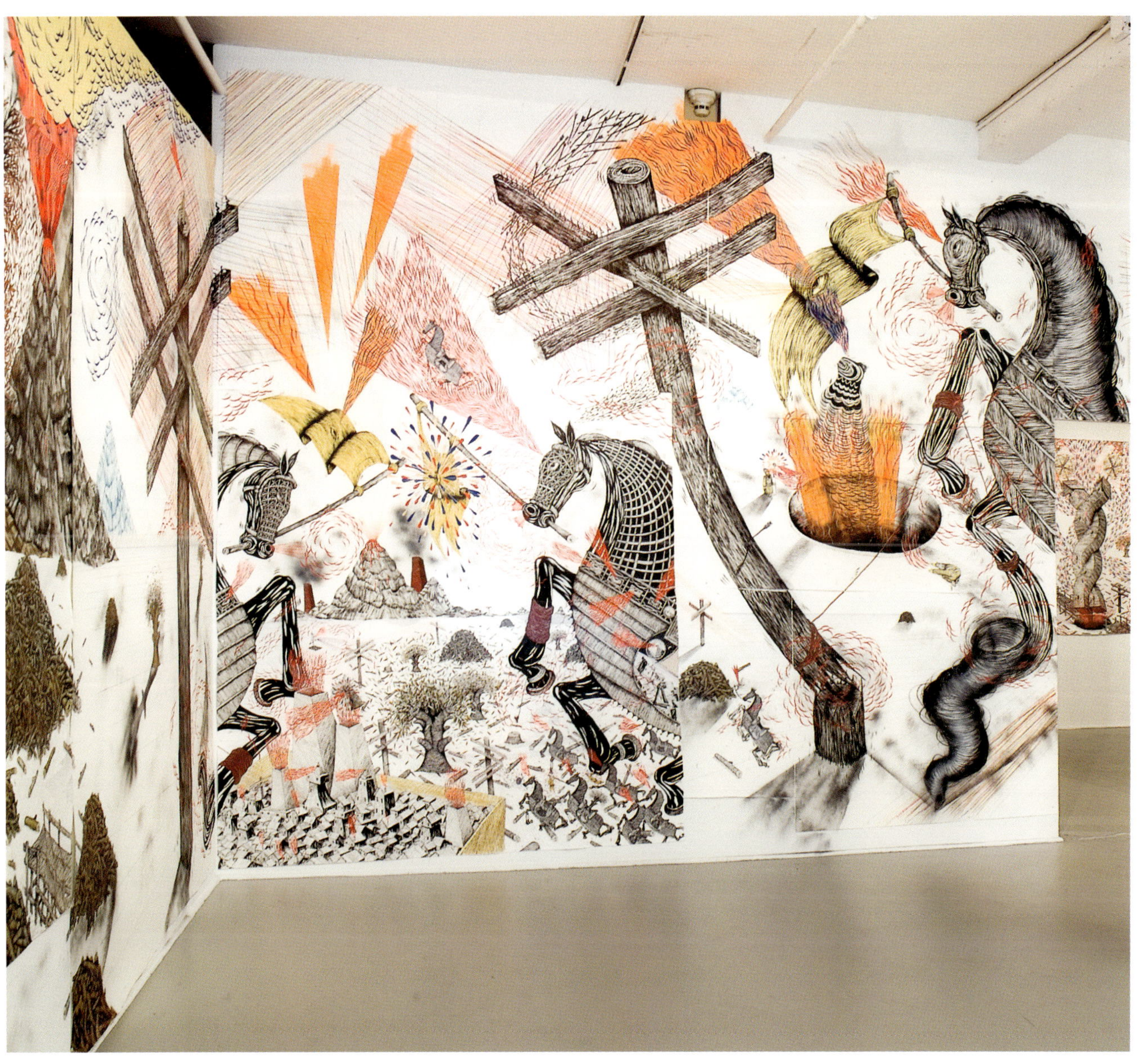

Andrew Schoultz, Installation view of *Motivational Baggage* at Boston Center for the Arts, 2006, mixed media on paper and drawn on the gallery wall, approximate dimensions 15 feet high and 30 feet wide. Photograph courtesy of the Artist.

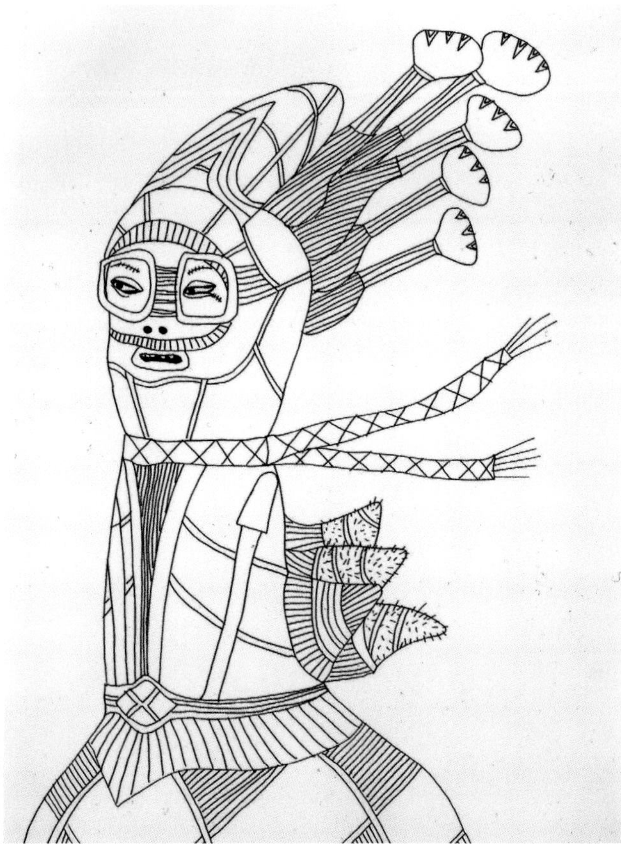

Laylah Ali, *Untitled*, 2004, ink on paper, 9 ½ x 7 ½ inches (LA 138). Courtesy of 303 Gallery, New York.

real physical conditions. Barry McGee, Clare Rojas, Chris Johanson, and Andrew Schoultz, for example, are political advocates associated with the so-called "Mission School."[38] While addressing such issues as drug abuse, homelessness, and urban decay, they manage to maintain their senses of humor and their affection for their neighbors, despite all the dereliction they see on the streets around them. As recognized artists, they are invited to write (and draw) their works on the interior walls of galleries and art museums. As graffiti artists, they surreptitiously decorate (or deface and vandalize) buildings in the Mission District of San Francisco.[39] They tell their stories, not only through traditional techniques learned in art school, but also through found objects, appropriated texts, and spray-painted walls and automobiles. They use both the acceptable practices of the establishment and the outlaw practices of local, indigenous cultures.

McGee is well-known in the San Francisco community by his street name "Twist." His untitled drawing in *Running around the Pool* depicts one of his stock down-and-out characters, a hobo-like figure who is at least partly a self-portrait. Such figures are ubiquitous in McGee's work and often appear in his murals and in his decorations on cars and trucks. They also appear in his wall ensembles of empty liquor bottles and his collections of framed images.[40] In the drawing here under discussion, McGee writes a series of words around the edges in his characteristic script. Such texts are hard to read and hard to interpret, except by connoisseurs of graffiti. Also included in the exhibition are seven of McGee's decorated found images, which include a photograph, some drawings, and some abstract tile patterns. These are placed together in a tight grouping. Such salon-style arrangements are used by several artists associated with the Mission School. They can go into and around corners and be quite extensive. Rojas, for example, sometimes arranges her works in this manner, as does Johanson. These groupings can also suggest ex-votos, an association that is perhaps particularly germane to the cultural context of Mission School art, given that there is a large Mexican-American population living in the Mission District.[41]

Rojas creates seemingly mythological settings and populates them with fantastic, cartoon-like characters. In *Untitled (Woman Holding Flower)*, a flat, apparently winged human figure floats near floral patterns. This design seems innocuous until we notice the bizarre scale and the animals standing on the leaves. The uneasiness that such a work engenders is characteristic of her approach. Rojas's drawings share this edgy quality with other Mission School works including those produced by Margaret Kilgallen.[42] They also have much in common with the kind of imagery produced earlier by Chicago Imagists such as Karl Wirsum.[43] Especially in her installations, which can at first seem like nurseries, Rojas creates scary environments where little children encounter strange, sometimes threatening, creatures. In addition to being a multitalented visual artist, Rojas is a musician and has formed a band. The songs that she composes and plays for/as "Peggy Honeywell" also have an unaccountably haunting quality, and their lyrics can be thought of as subtexts or accompaniments to her installations.[44]


38    See Glen Helfand, "The Mission School," *San Francisco Bay Guardian*, July 26, 2002; available online at http://www.sfbg.com/36/28/art_mission_school.html; for a discussion of several younger artists now working in the San Francisco Mission District, most of whom draw abstractly, see Lawrence Rinder, "Learning at the Mission School," *Parkett*, no. 74 (2005): 186-90.

39    Johanson now lives and works in Portland, Oregon; http://www.artnet.com/artist/9030/chris-johanson.htm.

40    See Eungie Joo, *Regards, Barry McGee*, exh. cat. (Minneapolis, Minn.: Walker Art Center, 1998); also Hoptman, "Comics and Other Subcultures," *Drawing Now* (cited n. 14), 129-30.

41    See Aaron Rose, "Least Likely to Succeed," in *Beautiful Losers: Contemporary Art and*

*Street Culture*, exh. cat., ed. Aaron Rose and Christian Strike (Cincinnati, Ohio: Contemporary Arts Center; San Francisco: Yerba Buena Center for the Arts, 2004), 31-47.

42    Margaret Kilgallen was a prominent member of the Mission School. She was married to Barry McGee and passed away of cancer in 2001 at the age of 33.

43    Rojas received her M.F.A. in 2002 from the School of the Art Institute of Chicago where Wirsum and other Chicago Imagists were on the faculty.

44    It's a little unclear whether or not "Peggy Honeywell" is the name of the band or Rojas's pseudonym. Maybe it's both. A number of Rojas's works are included in *Beautiful Losers: Contemporary Art and Street Culture*, exh. cat., ed. Aaron Rose and Christian Strike (Cincinnati, Ohio: Contemporary Arts Center; San Francisco: Yerba Buena Center for the Arts, 2004).

Like Rojas, Johanson is a musician and has played in several punk/noise bands in San Francisco. He is known for his faux-naïve works that are a cross between children's drawing and Ben Shahn social realism.[45] Johanson also paints quirky abstractions that he refers to as "energy bursts." In the drawing included in *Running around the Pool*, a number of multi-colored heads are clustered together. A speech bubble emerges from one of the faces saying "I am what is called human." Schoultz also emerges from the worlds of street art and alternative music. He uses what he calls a "repertoire of iconic images" to create complex, large-scale environments. "Through murals, paintings, installations, and drawings, I have used these images to tell stories about everyday life in America, filtering political commentary through the forms of graffiti art and underground comics, fused with clip-art from the early 1900s and medieval renderings that chart the history of man and nature."[46]

The raw approaches used by Mission School artists develop out of alternative music scenes, and they are related to the marginalized traditions of surfing and skateboarding.[47] The impacts of independent magazines and underground comics are also apparent in the work of many Mission School artists. Heroic early figures such as Robert Crumb, Victor Moscoso, and S. Clay Wilson, who drew for such magazines as *Zap Comix*, are much admired.[48] There is often a haphazard, improvisational quality in the work of these artists. Speaking of various subcultures including punk rock, hip-hop, graffiti, and street fashion, Christian Strike argues that the "DIY, or do-it-yourself, ethic was the overriding *modus operandi* that dominated each culture, and thus it provided a common perspective and aesthetic between them."[49] For the Mission School artists, the most important thing is to engage fervently with the world of lived experience.

The same could be said for New York based street artist Swoon. She uses this tag name, both to protect her anonymity, and to avoid prosecution for her interventions into public spaces. Like the Mission School artists, she deals with events unfolding on city streets, both in New York and around the world, but unlike them, she forgoes a cartoon-derived style in favor of a more illustrational approach. Her large, often life-sized drawings and wood-block prints are realistically executed, then cut into diverse forms and reassembled. They are sometimes installed in gallery spaces, but are more frequently placed directly in outdoor settings where they are allowed to deteriorate over time. Swoon works in an intermediate artistic domain somewhere between those of McGee and Natrop. The graffiti-inspired artists here under discussion—Swoon, Twist (McGee), Johanson, Rojas, and Schoultz—adopt manifold pictorial strategies. They employ words and images, cartoon exaggerations and realistic renderings, found objects and aggressive collage materials; and their drawings range from impenetrable

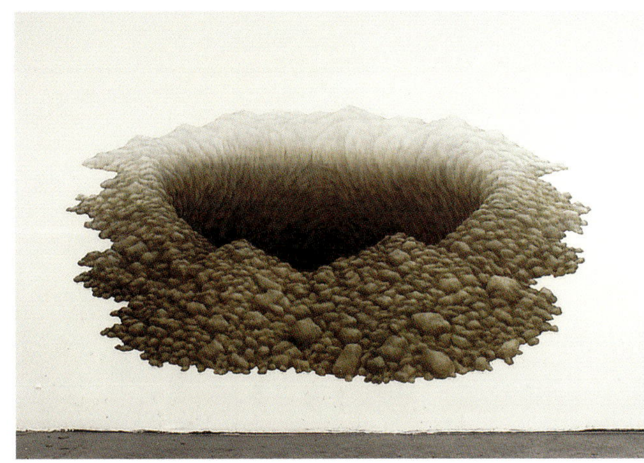

Gina Ruggeri, *Hole*, 2005, acrylic on mylar, 42 x 82 inches. Courtesy of the Artist and Kevin Bruk Gallery, Miami.

displays of pictorial and verbal information to succinct iconic (and ironic) statements. Their subject matters span self-delusion, personal resiliency, survival, boredom, self-satisfaction, disfiguration . . .

Many of the artists in *Running around the Pool* are obviously aware of ongoing theoretical debates in contemporary criticism, and their drawings reflect that awareness. They are also obviously aware of various outsider traditions. Perhaps the disjunctions between these high and low influences allow them to more effectively question the nature of art making. As a case in point, there are those artists who eschew draftsmanship as it has been conceived and taught in art schools, and their denunciation of "skill" can be seen in the way they use techniques derived from non-traditional sources. The street art and underground comics used by McGee, Rojas, Johanson, and Schoultz are examples. Their works—like many others in the current exhibition—reflect this generation's willingness to nose around in the murkier areas of contemporary society. These artists like to explore not only the "low," shadowy domains of popular culture, but also the more marginal areas of "high" culture. They are disposed to using methods formerly considered not quite good enough for the lofty enterprise of art making such as mechanical drawing, fashion illustration, computer-aided design, and architectural drafting. These techniques, and many others besides, are now welcomed as potential conceptual founts (and fonts).

45   Jack Hanley, "Chris Johanson—from Negation, Self-Help and Ron to Utopia and Center," in *Please Listen I Have Something to Tell You about What Is*, by Chris Johanson (New York: Alleged Press; Bologna: Damiani Editore, 2007), 114; see also Craig Garrett, "Art and Artlessness: The Emergence of the Professional Naïve," *Flash Art* 36 (May-June 2003): 130-33.

46   Andrew Schoultz, "Artist Statement," http://www.andrewschoultz.com/pages2/bio.htm.

47   Surfing and skateboarding are, of course, related practices. The skateboard was developed to replace the surfboard so that it could be used in places and at times that were inappropriate for surfing.

48   For good recent discussions of comic-inspired art, see *Splat Boom Pow! The Influence of Cartoons in Contemporary Art*, exh. cat. (Houston, Tex.: Contemporary Arts Museum,

2003), essays by Valerie Cassel, Robert Sabin, and Bernard Welt; *Comic Release! Negotiating Identity for a New Generation*, exh. cat. (Pittsburgh: Regina Gough Miller Gallery, Carnegie Mellon University, 2003), essays by Vicky Clark, Ana Merino, and Barbara Bloemink; see also *Comic Abstraction: Image-Breaking, Image-Making*, exh. cat. (New York: Museum of Modern Art, 2007), essay by Roxana Marcoci.

49   Christian Strike, "The Creators," in *Beautiful Losers: Contemporary Art and Street Culture*, exh. cat., ed. Aaron Rose and Christian Strike (Cincinnati, Ohio: Contemporary Arts Center; San Francisco: Yerba Buena Center for the Arts, 2004), 223-38, the quote is from p. 225; for a more theoretical study of some of the important historical roots of these impulses, see Dick Hebdige, *Subculture: The Meaning of Style* (London and New York: Methuen, 1979); also idem, *Hiding in the Light: On Images and Things* (London and New York: Routledge, 1987).

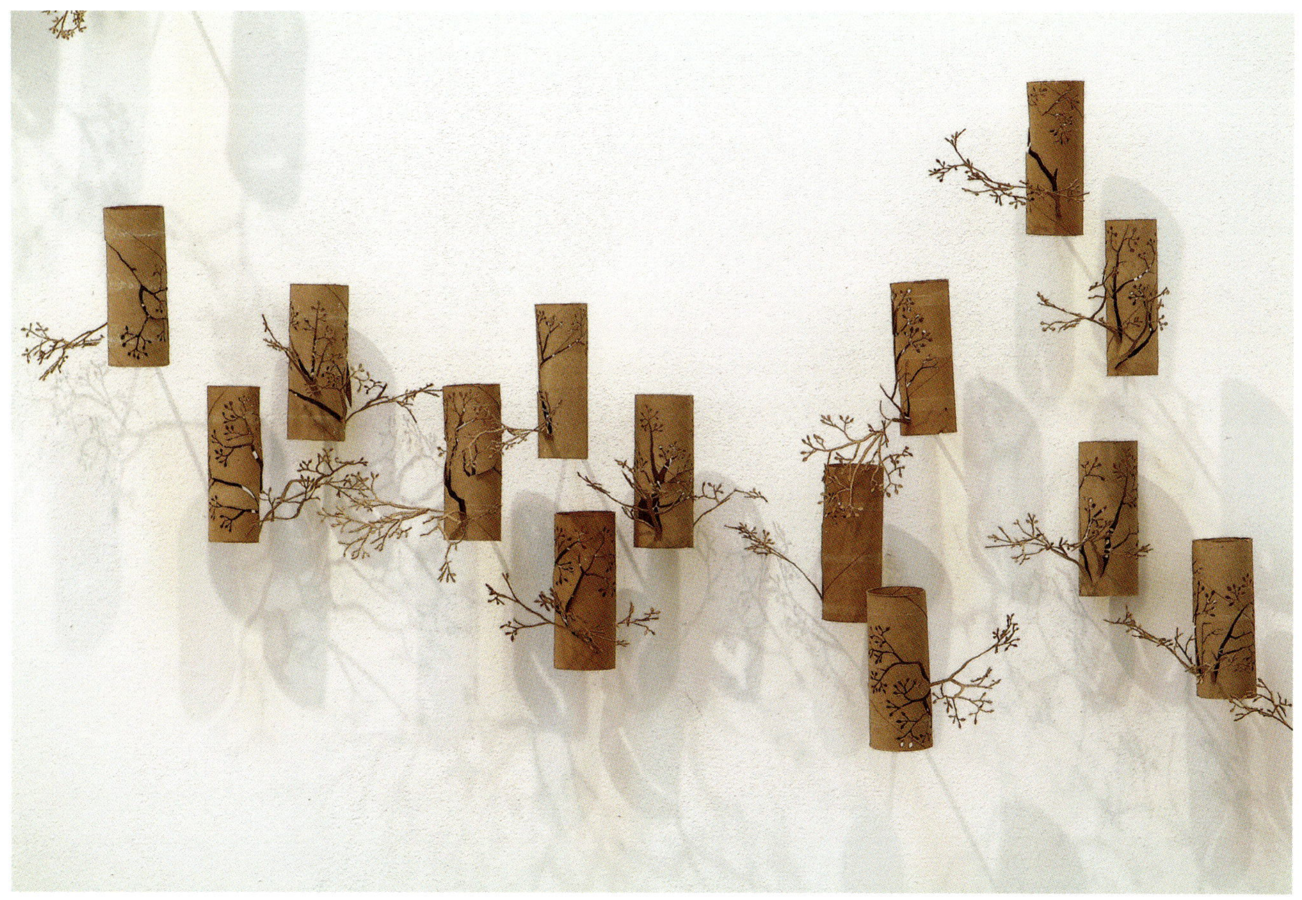

Yuken Teruya, installation photograph from *Light Year 2*, 2006, 22 paper rolls, magnets and nails, 23 x 63 x 10 inches. Collection of Glenn R. Fuhrman. Photograph courtesy of the Artist and Shoshana Wayne Gallery, Santa Monica, California.

Among the more conceptually oriented artists using practical "anti-skills" are "Los Carpinteros." This collective group of artists from Cuba includes Alexandre Arrechea, Marco Castillo, and Dagoberto Rodríguez.[50] They take their name from the Spanish word for "Carpenters" and think of themselves as much as artisans as artists: "Giving ourselves this name implied a sort of guild affiliation," one member of the group has said.[51] The group engages the built environment both in terms of its construction and its deconstruction, and their drawings generally depict some aspect of building practice. The resulting projects are ironic, and they make use of mixed metaphors, combining both architectural and non-architectural elements. The proposals put forth by Los Carpinteros are odd fusions, as if Jean-Jacques Lequeu had gotten together with Jorge Luis Borges.[52] In *Pool-Pool (Estudio Final)*, a swimming pool becomes a pool table. In *Alto Parlante—Cohiba*, a stack of audio equipment becomes a high-rise apartment complex, with the word play hinging on loud speakers, prohibition, and loud speaking. If such structures were actually built, they would be absurd. The drawings of Los Carpinteros are meditations on contemporary urban life. They reflect not only slums in Cuba, but also the blighted (and absurd) conditions that obtain in most cities of the world.[53] The conceptual approaches used by these artists, and the eccentricity of their images,

---

50    Los Carpinteros was formed in 1994. Their full names are Alexandre Jesus Arrechea Zambrano, Marco Antonio Castillo Valdés, and Dagoberto Rodríguez Sánchez. Arrechea left the group in 2003 and did not contribute to the drawings in *Running around the Pool*; see Charles Merewether, "Los Carpinteros," in *Vitamin D: New Perspectives in Drawing* (London and New York: Phaidon Press, 2005), 56; see also *Los Carpinteros: provisorische Utopien*, exh. cat. (Aachen, Germany: Ludwig Forum für Internationale Kunst, 1998), essay by Eugenio Valdés Figueroa, translated into German by Anja Geiger.

51    Alexandre Arrechea quoted by Rosa Lowinger, "The Object as Protagonist: An Interview with Los Carpinteros, Alexandre Arrechea, Marco Castillo, and Dagoberto Rodriguez," *Sculpture* 18 (December 1999): 24-31, the quote in from p. 25.

52    In addition to Lequeu, Hoptman suggests Étienne-Louis Boullée and Claude-Nicolas Ledoux, as well as the prison designs of Jeremy Bentham, as possible sources of inspiration for Los Carpinteros; see her chapter, "Drafting an Architecture," *Drawing Now* (cited n. 14), 49.

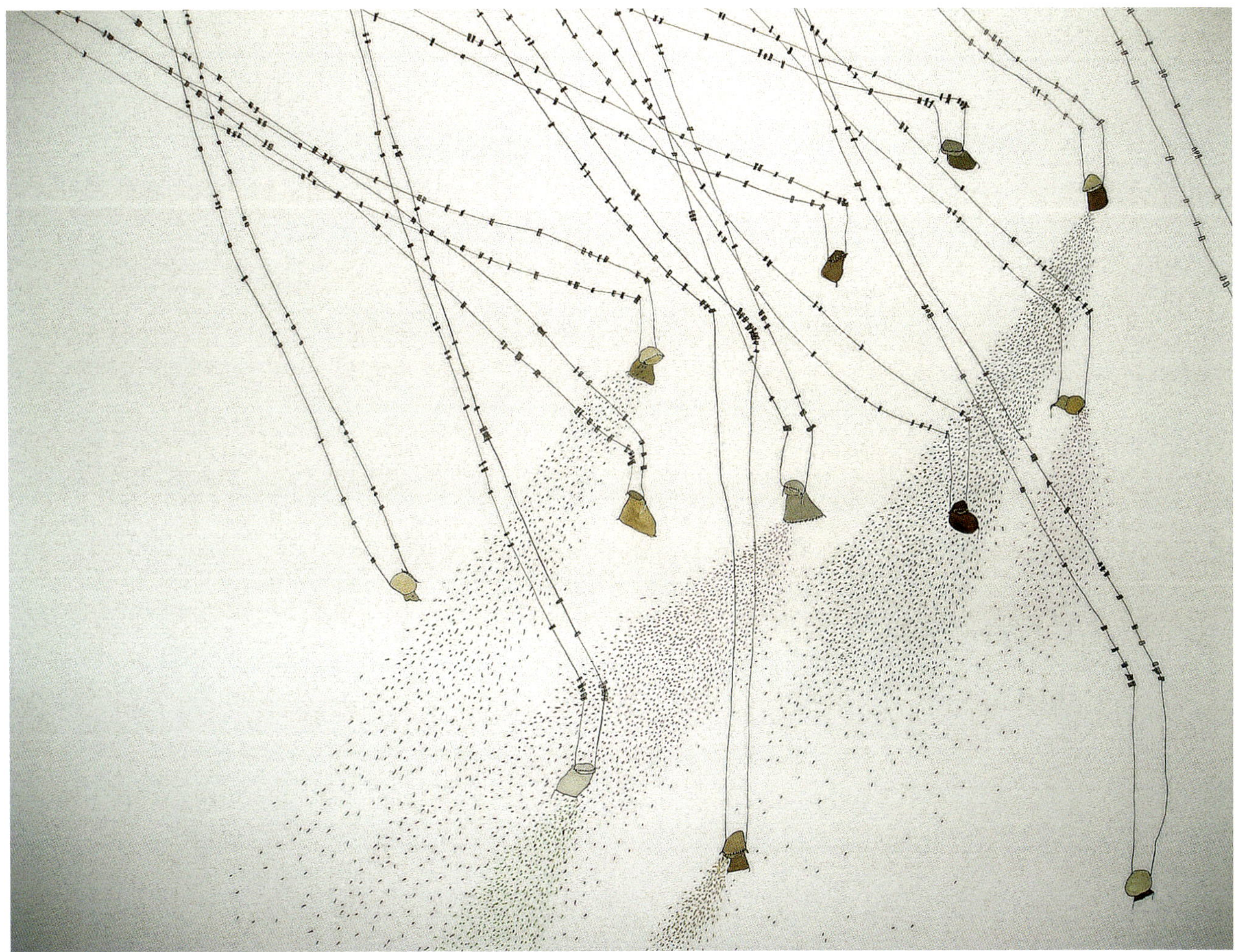

Amy Rathbone, *Rainbags*, 2005, ink and gouache on paper, 22 x 30 inches. Courtesy of the Artist and Gregory Lind Gallery, San Francisco. On loan from Priska Juschka Fine Art, New York.

put representation *per se* in an unusual light. Especially when achieved through economic design processes, representation can suddenly seem all too politically motivated and unstable.

With this point in mind, obvious sources of inspiration for many of the works in *Running around the Pool* can be found in Pop Art, which is an art movement that also makes what is ordinary seem extraordinary. This said, however, the possible connections between Pop Art and the drawings in the current exhibition are rarely straightforward. The complications may reflect contemporary artists being more critical, or at least, more attentive to critical matters, than were their Pop Art precursors. Raymond Pettibon

has made this point succinctly with regard to his own work:

> What the Pop artists did by co-opting the language of commercialism for their own "different, appealing" art was honest and new. When I started copying from TV, movies, or magazines, however, I had no illusions I was doing anything original. I wasn't even trying to be ironic or kitsch. Comics and illustrations simply worked well as a universal means of expression. I didn't feel I had to revisit or belabor the idea of mechanical reproduction.[54]

---

53  See Mike Davis, "Planet of Slums," *New Left Review*, 2nd ser., no. 26 (March-April 2004): 5-34.

54  Raymond Pettibon interviewed by Jordan Kantor, "Raymond Pettibon," *Artforum International* 43 (October 2004): 174.

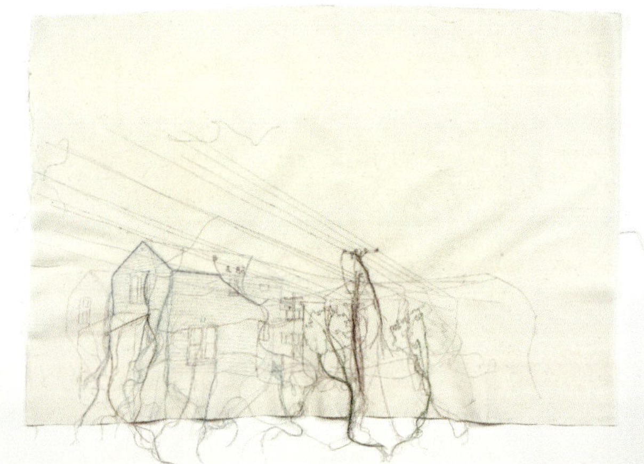

Tucker Schwarz, *Somehow it never seems to be quite enough*, 2005 thread on muslin, 24 x 36 inches. Courtesy of the Artist and Gregory Lind Gallery, San Francisco.

Like Pettibon, artists now accept sources from popular culture without feeling any need to be defensive, but neither are they uninformed about them. In Pettibon's words, "we already know representations, however feebly drawn, are still representations, and therefore illusions that delude both subjects and audience."[55] After comparing the artist to Johns, Lichtenstein, and Warhol, Benjamin H. D. Buchloh argues that

> Pettibon's response is not only directed at the relatively anodyne subject matter of these Pop artists, it is perhaps much more precisely addressing the sinuous elegance and the seemingly imperturbable linearity of their drawings. Against their placid acceptance of the cartooned forms of social interaction and articulation, Pettibon's drawings reinscribe the compulsive, fractured immediacy of the expressive notation made under duress, as if dictated by the urgency of the scenes of crime, violence, and obscenity that they try to come to terms with, as drawings."[56]

Not only Pettibon's drawing/writing combinations, but also the other Pop-inflected works in the current exhibition are savvy in just these ways. The artists are less drawn to advertising emblems as cultural signs than they are interested in them as examples of linguistic complexity. They are indifferent to, or suspicious of, the aesthetics of such forms, and

they doubt the facts presupposed by them. Allowing their works to have a cartoon-like quality provides the artists with access to the trivial as well as to the traumatic dimensions of ordinary experience. The accessibility is the main point. The Pop artists took ordinary things, things that had not been included in the world of art, and dealt with how they were evaluated and valued by ordinary people. They used this material to talk about everyday life in high art terms. In contemporary practice, the celebratory side of Pop Art, the way in which it seemed to put forward a cheerful acceptance of commodity aesthetics, is no longer acceptable. What makes today's homes "so different" is no longer "so appealing."[57]

Despite a pervasive skepticism hovering over contemporary works of art, we, as viewers, are still driven to unlock their secrets. Perhaps we are urged to do so because visual representations provide us with such rich domains for analysis. This generalization seems particularly true of the drawings in *Running around the Pool*. Their content can sometimes be discovered by appealing to their use of language. In some cases, as we have seen with Pettibon, Johanson, and McGee, texts are combined with images. In other cases, the only texts available are the titles. But through these titles, we can sometimes narrow down the possibilities. For example, Natrop's *Fern Space Burst*, Johanson's *Untitled (I Am What Is Called Human)*, and Crotty's *Vineyard Potential* suggest directions for us to follow. We can enter into the provinces alluded to by the titles, although we may be surprised by what we find. The real wonder of this situation is that the artists are, in fact, running around an immense pool of resources, and they can dive in at any point, swim in any direction, and dive to any depth, even though the sign says: "No *Running around the Pool*." And so can we. As viewers, we can join with the artists in sending messages back and forth, in telling stories, and in complaining to one another about the human predicament. We can use whatever terms we wish. Especially by bringing into play popular culture, we can access the almost infinite stockpiles of images and texts that are there, in a sense crying out for appropriation and restatement. Any image, any text, can be taken up and transformed into whatever new configuration we deem necessary.

Invented worlds and fanciful spaces are especially prevalent in *Running around the Pool*. Chloe Piene's charcoal drawings on vellum recall both Egon Schiele and Francisco Goya. She renders emaciated body fragments that seem to float within a welter of line segments. Her body parts (and bones) are suspended, like contemporary "disasters of war," or perhaps a little less graphically, like the "caprichos" of postmodern incompleteness. However they are taken, the gracefulness of her drawings belies their suggestions of violence and morbidity.[58] Paul Rutkovsky's media-inspired drawings suggest Saturday morning children's programming gone horribly wrong. In a riotous kind of way, they combine parody and critique, creating arcane narratives apparently drawn from the usual vernacular suspects like animated television shows and movies.[59] Kirsten Rae

55     Ibid.

56     Benjamin H. D. Buchloh, "Raymond Pettibon: Return to Disorder and Disfiguration," *October*, no. 92 (Spring 2000): 37-51.

57     Richard Hamilton's famous collage, *Just What Is It that Makes Today's Homes So Different, So Appealing?*, was used in the design of the poster for the exhibition *This Is Tomorrow* held at the Whitechapel Art Gallery in London in 1956. For an insightful analysis that puts this exhibition into context, and in terms relevant to the present discussion, see David Robbins, "The Independent Group: Forerunners of Postmodernism?" in *The Independent Group:*

*Postwar Britain and the Aesthetics of Plenty*, ed. David Robbins (Cambridge, Mass., and London: MIT Press, 1990), 237-48.

58     Frances Roberts, "Chloe Piene," *Artforum International* 41 (May 2003): 168-69; and Maika Pollack, "Chloe Piene," *Flash Art* 36 (May-June 2003): 90; see also Barry Schwabsky, "Chloe Piene," in *Vitamin D: New Perspectives in Drawing* (London and New York: Phaidon Press, 2005), 256.

59     Paul Rutkovsky, http://mailer.fsu.edu/~prutkov/top.html.

Simonsen's drawings seem at first to be renderings of harmless domestic scenes. But on closer inspection, works such as *Running Scared* and *Special Day* become ominous. "My work is concerned with transgression and debasement," she says. "I find inspiration in the more menacing rhymes and stories from traditional children's books such as Mother Goose, as well as Victorian era English school books."[60] Marcel Dzama's drawings fall into a similar category: at first, they recall illustrations for fairy tales, but they soon disclose their darker side. In *Eight Strong Winds*, the work included in *Running around the Pool*, trees sprout eight balletic female riflemen (strong winds?) and support bedridden figures. The trunks expand into demonic shapes and the branches harbor much-too-large songbirds. As we examine Dzama's seemingly inoffensive picture, in reveals a brutal world of torment and persecution, a fantasy land that is all too close to the nefarious goings-on of the real world.[61]

The French poststructuralist philosopher Gilles Deleuze might have called the drawings in *Running around the Pool* "nomadic." The approach he had in mind traces a shattered image of existence. It depicts a ruined world picture and gives it back to us as mirror surface. As pointed out earlier, the various kinds of drawing seen in the current exhibition are analytical and self-reflexive as well as intuitive. They are almost always partially undefined representations whose subjects are decentered, as if returned to our visual systems after being reflected from curved and distorted surfaces. They subvert authority, turn hierarchy on its head, disrupt stability, and set clarity and structure in motion. By so doing, they multiply our points of view, opening our eyes to other ways of seeing. Deleuze describes a complex kind of visual representation in which our making a determination, or a distinction, is closely linked to the indeterminate and the indistinct:

> Every object, every thing, must see its own identity swallowed up in difference, each being no more than a difference between differences. Difference must be shown *differing*. We know that modern art tends to realize these conditions: in this sense it becomes a veritable *theatre* of metamorphoses and permutations. A theatre where nothing is fixed, a labyrinth without a thread (Ariadne has hung herself).[62]

Many of the drawings in *Running around the Pool* involve such directionless meanderings, such contradictory determinations and distinctions, and they disclose highly differentiated pictorial spaces.

Amy Rathbone's drawings engage such spaces. They have a delicate insubstantiality. She sometimes uses ephemeral materials, or perhaps better, materials that suggest the ephemeral, like tea and coffee

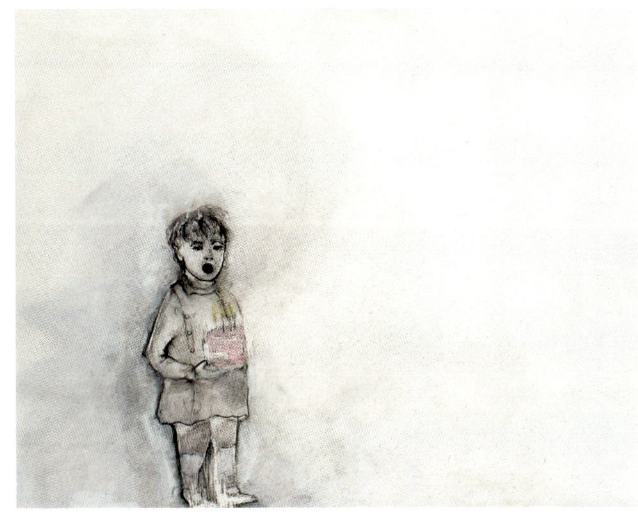

Kirsten Rae Simonsen, *Special Day*, 2007, charcoal, pencil, acrylic, and gesso on wood panel, 11 x 14 inches. Courtesy of the Artist.

stains. Her elusive and light-hearted works seem recondite, an impression reinforced by her titles such as *Rainbags*. In her installations like *Plebians*, wispy lines drawn directly on walls and small areas of dripping spray paint mingle with shadows cast by wires coming out from the wall surfaces, creating a perceptual oscillation between the material and immaterial elements of the work.[63] Robyn O'Neil's drawings also seem to depict esoteric domains, but hers are dark and brooding. The frightening worlds that she creates recall half-forgotten nightmares. Her titles, such as *Masses and Masses Rove a Darkened Pool, Never Is there Laughter on the Ship of Fools* and *This Is a Descending World*, reinforce the dystopian implications of her threat-filled topographies. As James Yood has suggested, "in the absence of the laws and ideas that make up civilization, O'Neil sees a potential release of savagery, a kind of disorientation of place that reveals mankind's often horrific tendencies."[64] Laura Owens' works can also seem obscure, and they can have their dark side. In her case, this quality may have to do with her use of decorative elements such as patterned and embroidered fabrics. Her paintings and drawings are always untitled and they rarely have specific subject matters. Nevertheless, they do have a residual anecdotal quality, although our being able to find any kind of plot, or a narrative thread, is probably hopeless. But, as she says, "a painting can offer up any number of options for meaning," and the same can be said for her drawings.[65] The two watercolors in the present exhibition seem to depict mutated landscapes, one with twisted toy-like

---


60    Kirsten Rae Simonsen, unpublished artist's statement (provided by Florida State University).

61    Andrea K. Scott, "Marcel Dzama," in *Vitamin D: New Perspectives in Drawing* (London and New York: Phaidon Press, 2005), 90; see also Edward Leffingwell, "Marcel Dzama," *Art in America* 89 (February 2001): 144-45.

62    Gilles Deleuze, *Difference and Repetition*, trans. Paul Patton (New York: Columbia University Press, 1994), 56. For a useful discussion of Deleuze, see Dorothea Olkowski, "Difference and the Ruin of Representation in Gilles Deleuze," in *Sites of Vision: The Discursive Construction of Sight in the History of Philosophy*, ed. David Michael Levin (Cambridge, Mass., and London: MIT Press, 1997), 467-91.

63    Stephanie Cash, "Amy Rathbone," *Art in America* 94 (May 2006): 186-87.

64    James Yood, "Robyn O'Neil," *Artforum International* 42 (Summer 2004): 253.

65    Susan Morgan, "A Thousand Words: Laura Owens Talks about Her New Work," *Artforum International* 37 (Summer 1999): 131.

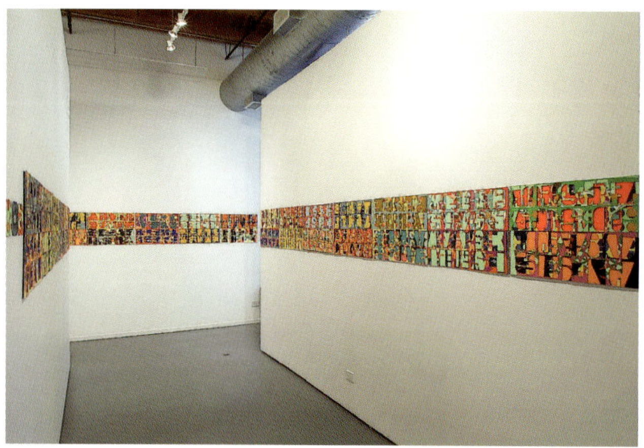

Pae White, *The Sea, The Sea and Everything in Between*, 2006, cut silkscreen paper collage, 8 1/2 x 24 inches each panel, installation view from *Midnight*, Skestos-Gabriele Gallery, Chicago. Photograph courtesy of Skestos-Gabriele Gallery, Chicago, and 1301 PE, Los Angeles.

forms and disconnected eyeballs, the other with collage elements suggesting posts in the foreground and a beehive structure with collage elements suggesting a Dutch windmill floating in the middle distance. These drawings hint that something weird is going on, and this presentiment is obscurely reinforced by their ornamentality. Owens' often ambiguous works, which occupy positions somewhere between being ingenuous and sarcastic, between emulating kitsch doilies and reprising color-field painting, wind up celebrating, although in a vaguely sinister way, the rich and often outlandish conditions of contemporary (post-)postmodern life.[66]

Another word that could be applied to much of the work in *Running around the Pool* is "surreal." And the artist in the exhibition who is most closely associated with surrealism is Louise Bourgeois. Her drawings are often ideational sketches closely associated with her sculpture, and the work included in the current exhibition is a case in point.[67] It seems to be a working drawing for one of her hybrid forms, the kind that make viewers, especially male viewers, very uncomfortable. Experiencing such works, we often "come full circle in the psychological labyrinth that Bourgeois entices us to enter with her strange but somehow primordial images."[68] We encounter them in terms of their inherent ambiguity and

our own ambiguous feelings about them. In her sculptures, Bourgeois often combines abstract and figurative elements. In the small sketch included in this show, she merges organic and architectural forms, suggesting that it may be in the lineage of her "Femmes-maisons."[69] In sculptures related to the drawing, eggs and seed pods seem to metastasize into sepulchers and skulls. Bourgeois once remarked that her drawings were "ideas and little complaints,"[70] but they can also be powerful reminders of the themes she addresses in her sculpture, themes that include sexual awakening, love, hate, birth, and death. The works of Laylah Ali could also be described in these terms, although her ideas and the issues she complains about are not exactly "little." Her works, like those of Bourgeois, engage universal themes. Her aesthetic sensibility owes a great deal to comic books, but her drawings and paintings are anything but funny. Her characters, with their basketball and dodge-ball heads, wearing their exotic costumes, refer to the most disturbing aspects of social discord and ethnic violence.[71]

The rather odd though distinctive version of realism that informs comics and cartoons is not the only approach to representation evident in *Running around the Pool*. Gina Ruggeri's drawings consist of tightly rendered ordinary objects such as mounds overgrown by dense vegetation in *Overgrowth* and piles of rocks around an excavation in *Hole*. A typical work of hers is drawn on Mylar, cut, and then attached directly to a wall surface. "Because it is removed from the traditional frame of the rectangle," Ruggeri explains, "the image often appears as an illusionary object that floats in the white space of the wall, hovering in a continuum of physical and pictorial space."[72] Her approach gives illusionism an unreal, if not surreal, quality. The works of Tucker Schwarz also involve ordinary scenes, and they too are eccentric. She often depicts architectural vistas such as empty city streets. She sews such images onto muslin supports, allowing surplus threads to hang down from their surfaces. These delicately sewn drawings convey a sense of loss and sterility, as well as an impression that they are incomplete or in progress.[73] The titles Schwarz assigns to her images amplify their bleakness: *Nothing Can Save Me Now, Somehow It Never Seems to Be Quite Enough*, and *Well, I Suppose That Explains Everything*. The constructions of Yuken Teruya are also fragile and desolate. He is particularly well-known for his renovations of discarded containers such as pizza delivery boxes and paper sacks. In *Light Year 2*, he cuts the shapes of small plants from discarded paper rolls. In these branching forms, the cellulose in the cardboard seems to have somehow reasserted its original organic pattern and become once again part of a living thing. *Notice Forest (Graz Zweitausenddrei)*, the work included in *Running around the Pool*, is from a series of works with the same general title, "Notice Forest." In


66    See *Laura Owens*, exh. cat. (Los Angeles: Museum of Contemporary Art, 2003), essays by Thomas Lawson and Paul Schimmel; also Carmine Iannaccone, "Entertainment Complex," *Frieze*, no. 49 (November-December 1999): 88-91; and Hoptman, "Ornament and Crime: Toward Decoration," *Drawing Now* (cited n. 14), 31-32.

67    There are some interesting exceptions to this rule such as the series of drawings that Bourgeois did during a period when she was unable to sleep; see *Louise Bourgeois: The Insomnia Drawings*, 2 vols. (Zurich: Daros, in collaboration with Peter Blum Edition, New York, and Scalo, Zurich, Berlin, and New York, 2000), texts by Marie-Laure Bernadac and Elisabeth Bronfen.

68    Robert Storr, "I Am I Because . . .," in *Art 21: Art in the Twenty-First Century*, vol. 1 (New York: Abrams, 2001), 130.

69    Marie-Laure Bernadac, *Louise Bourgeois*, trans. Deke Dusinberre (Paris: Flammarion, 2006), 64-68: "The *Femmes maisons* ("house women") are perhaps emblematic of Louise

Bourgeois's entire oeuvre. The combination of geometric and organic forms, of rigidity and malleability, of architecture and viscera, serves as a metaphor for her own psychic makeup" (p. 64).

70    Press release for "Drawings by Louise Bourgeois," St. Louis Art Museum, St. Louis, Mo., March-June 2004.

71    See Suzanne Wise, "Musing the Muse: Looking at Laylah Ali's *Greenheads*," in *Laylah Ali*, exh. cat. (Boston: Institute of Contemporary Art, 2001), 7-11.

72    Gina Ruggeri, http://www.re.title.com/artists/Gina-Ruggeri.asp.

73    Schwarz's works are included in *By Hand: The Use of Craft in Contemporary Art*, ed. Shu Hung and Joseph Magliaro (New York: Princeton Architectural Press, 2007), 132-36.

these sculpture/drawings, Teruya cuts out the shape of a tree from one side of a paper sack and then suspends the delicate form inside the sack using string. The resulting landscape contained in the bag, with its small, insubstantial ecosystem, becomes an interactive theatrical set where such large issues as the impact of global economic expansion can be staged.[74] In his diminutive environments, the contradictions of late capitalism are eloquently displayed, although in a way that is not easily seen.

Merleau-Ponty once argued that our perceptions are formed as much by what lies hidden on all sides as by what lies before us. Taking the paintings of Paul Cézanne as his point of departure, he contended that the artist helps us discover those things we normally overlook, the objects that are lost in the noise of day-to-day experience. As a noetic-noematic act, epitomized by the probing methods of Cézanne, painting makes visible what is invisible.[75] The theoretical approach of Merleau-Ponty is applicable to many of the works in *Running around the Pool*. The searching quality that we see in images, such as the small sack by Teruya, often depends upon open spaces, interruptions, breaks, and pauses in their compositions and conceptualizations. The interstices in such works not only suggest divisions between basic elements, but also intervals between disparate cultural deployments. In the clearings opened up in these works, although they still manifest distant tracts of modernism, especially those that can be traced from Post-Impressionism to Abstract Expressionism, something more is there as well. We not only see echoes of automatism and spontaneity, but also hear reverberations of despair and schizophrenia. In these new drawings, we encounter a space filled with the noise and debris of modernity collapsing under its own weight.

The involutions recorded by the artists in *Running around the Pool* were sketched against a cultural background of dissolution. The drawings in the show resist following rules, welcome diversity, and include much that was once excluded from the world of art. Much contemporary art is not only neo-conceptual but also hyper-conceptual. It takes for granted all kinds of appropriationism. It deals with contingency and fragmentation. The present condition of art carries with it an assumption that artists can make use of ready-made categories—both actual and conceptual—in any way they see fit. Such artistic concept/object entities can serve any purpose whatsoever. Emancipated practitioners thus recognize no limits to what they use in the construction of their works of art. The new avant-garde is no longer bound by any restraint, nor is it constrained to follow any course. This freedom can be seen either as a welcome release or as an invitation to disaster. The admiration for the historical avant-garde that characterizes some accounts of postmodernism has a conservative cast. Likewise, the use of recognizable imagery by many of the artists in *Running around the Pool* adheres to traditional methods and approaches. But as a response to years of rarified abstraction, this way of working is inevitable, and necessary. Even very familiar imagery can be difficult to understand, especially when it is put into new contexts and used for new purposes.

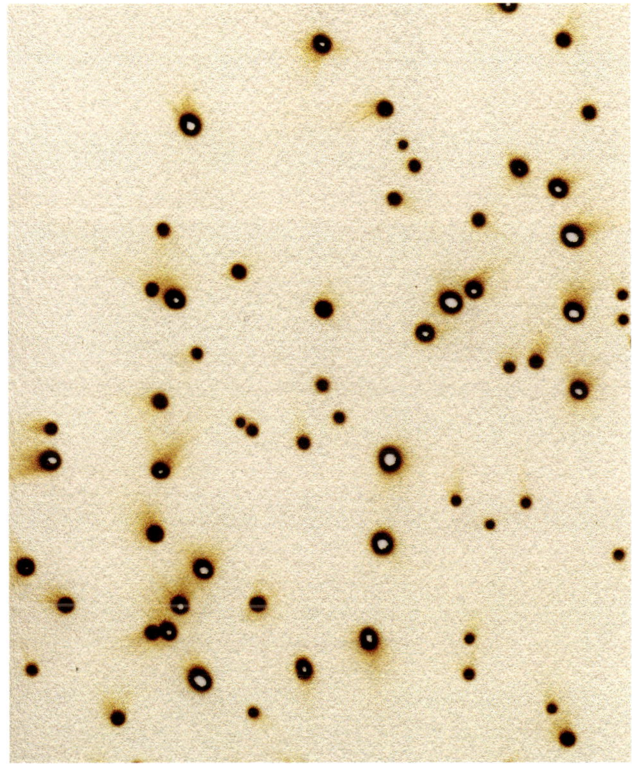

Wendy Wischer, *Sunspot diaries*, 2003, paper burned with magnifying glass and sunlight, 30 x 40 inches. Courtesy of the Artist and David Castillo Gallery, Miami.

In a recent discussion of contemporary drawing, Laura Hoptman argues that many artists have traditionally focused on the "process" of drawing. She quotes Richard Serra's statement that "drawing is a verb." In contrast, she suggests that many artists working today, including those in the exhibition she curated, feel that "drawing is not a verb, but a noun."[76] I would like to propose that, while these points are well taken, the contemporary situation in drawing is more complicated still. The word "drawing" is a verbal—a verb form used as another part of speech. More specifically, it is a gerund—a present participle used as a noun. In the grammar of contemporary practice, "drawing" can have both conjugations and declensions. It indexes not only the indicative and subjunctive moods, but also the nominative, accusative, dative, ablative, and genitive cases. The diverse forms taken by the grammar of contemporary art may have something to do with its grammatical elements being spread out to the far edges of practice where they diverge. The older conventions that

---

74    Andrea Inselmann, "Yuken Teruya," *Material Matters*, exh. cat. (Ithaca, N.Y.: Herbert F. Johnson Museum of Art, Cornell University, 2005), 62-65.

75    Maurice Merleau-Ponty, "Cézanne's Doubt," trans. Michael B. Smith, in *The Merleau-Ponty Aesthetics Reader: Philosophy and Painting*, ed. Galen A. Johnson and Michael B. Smith (Evanston, Ill.: Northwestern University Press, 1993), 59-75.

76    Hoptman, "Drawing Is a Noun," *Drawing Now* (cited n. 14), 12. For a discussion of the process aspects of drawing, see Pamela M. Lee, "Some Kinds of Duration: The Temporality of Drawing as Process Art," in *Afterimage: Drawing through Process*, exh. cat., ed. Cornelia H. Butler (Los Angeles: Museum of Contemporary Art; Cambridge, Mass., and London: MIT Press, 1999), 25-48.

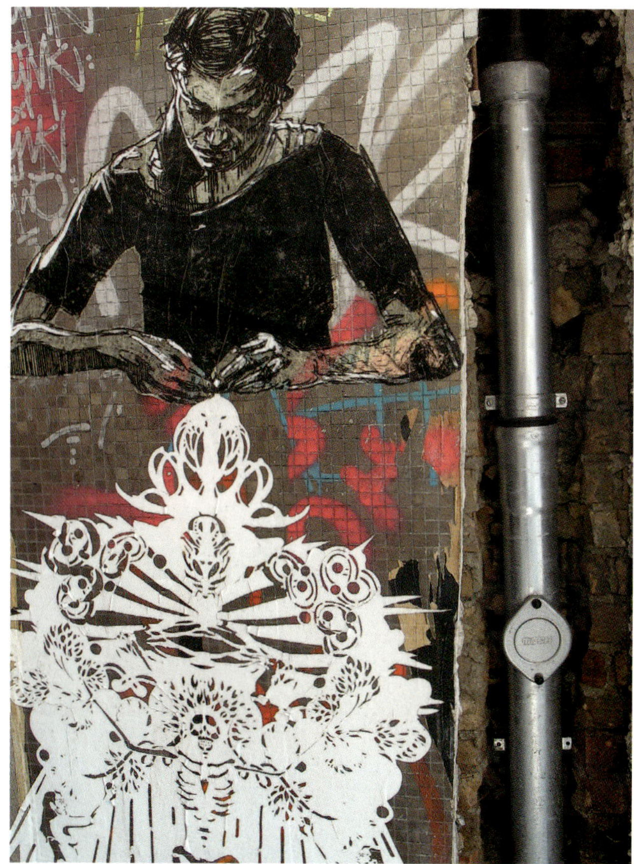

Swoon, *Allison, the Lace Maker*, 2004, relief print and cut paper, Berlin, Germany.

we have used to distinguish art media one from the other—say drawing from painting and painting from sculpture—no longer hold. Most of the works in *Running around the Pool* occupy grammatical areas for which we have no paradigms.

The artists exhibiting in *Running around the Pool* often seem uninterested in setting particular goals or establishing specific standards. The way they execute their drawings can be as important as how the drawings wind up looking. In their methods, objectives are often occluded. In some cases, the work may be about the traditional roles drawing has played, such as capturing a specific moment or mediating a given design problem. In other cases, the work may be about the touch or feel of the artist. But beyond such formal considerations, the drawings may also possess an exorbitance, a quality that Jacques Derrida may have meant to suggest when he said: "It is as if seeing were forbidden in order to draw, as if one drew only on the condition of not seeing, as if the drawing were a declaration of love destined for or suited to the invisibility of the other—unless it were in fact born from seeing the other withdrawn from sight."[77] Contemporary artists, by referencing the insubstantial nature of experience, engage modern life. The insufficiency of events and the way meaning shifts and changes through external effects (and affects) is a primary concern in much present-day discourse. By focusing on surface (and surface reflection), artists can position themselves as both the authors and the subjects of their own work. They can look at themselves looking, and by so doing, dislocate themselves in relation to their art and to art in general. Contemporary drawings deal, not only with actualized resemblances and mute meanings, but also with categories of experience that are just beyond expression.

—C.A.

---

77    Derrida, *Memoirs of the Blind* (cited n. 36), 49. For an examination of this essay, see Robert Vallier, "Blindness and Invisibility: The Ruins of Self-Portraiture (Derrida's Re-reading of Merleau-Ponty)," in *Écart & Différance: Merleau-Ponty and Derrida on Seeing and Writing*, ed. M. C. Dillon (Atlantic Highlands, N.J.: Humanities Press, 1997), 191-207.

Laylah Ali

Louise Bourgeois

Russell Crotty

Marcel Dzama

Janae Easton

Chris Johanson

Los Carpinteros

Barry McGee

Julie Mehretu

Chris Natrop

Robyn O'Neil

Laura Owens

Raymond Pettibon

Chloe Piene

Amy Rathbone

Clare Rojas

Gina Ruggeri

Paul Rutkovsky

Andrew Schoultz

Tucker Schwarz

Kirsten Rae Simonsen

Kiki Smith

Swoon

Yuken Teruya

Pae White

Wendy Wischer

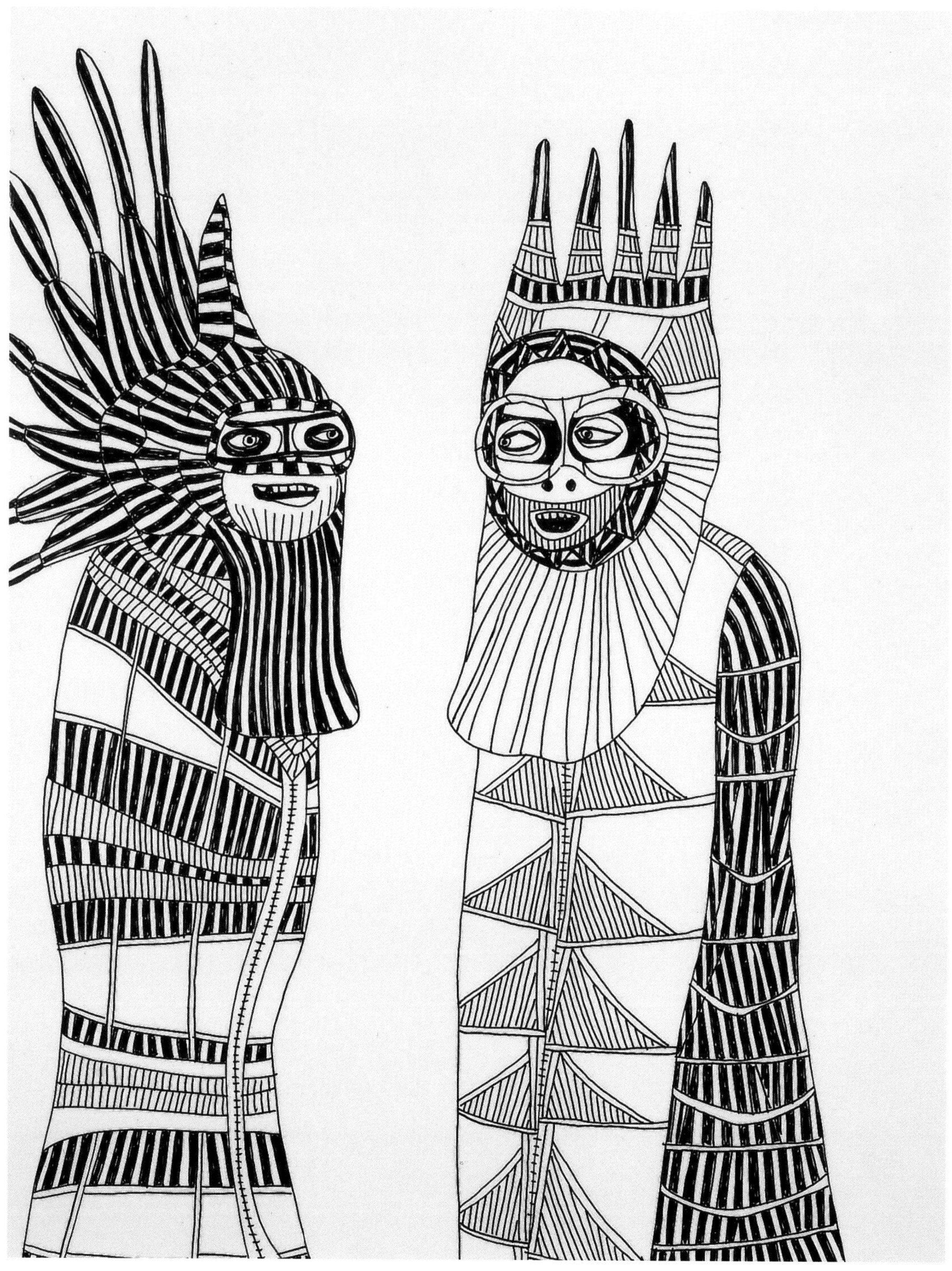

Laylah Ali, *Untitled*, 2004, ink on paper, 9 ½ x 7 ½ inches (LA 136). Courtesy of 303 Gallery, New York.

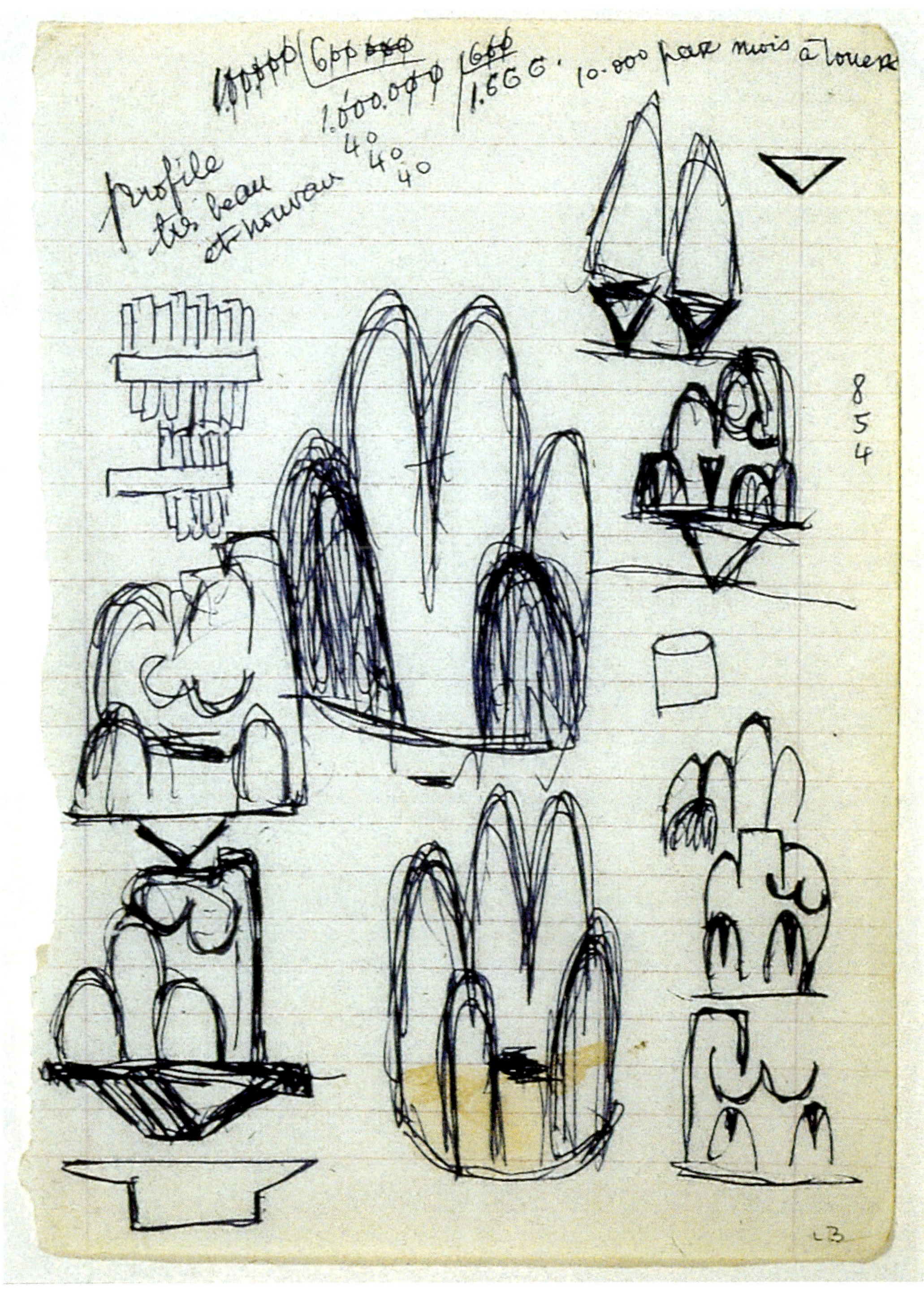

Louise Bourgeois, *Untitled*, 1971, ink on lined paper, 8 x 5 ¾ inches. Courtesy of the Artist and Cheim & Read, New York.

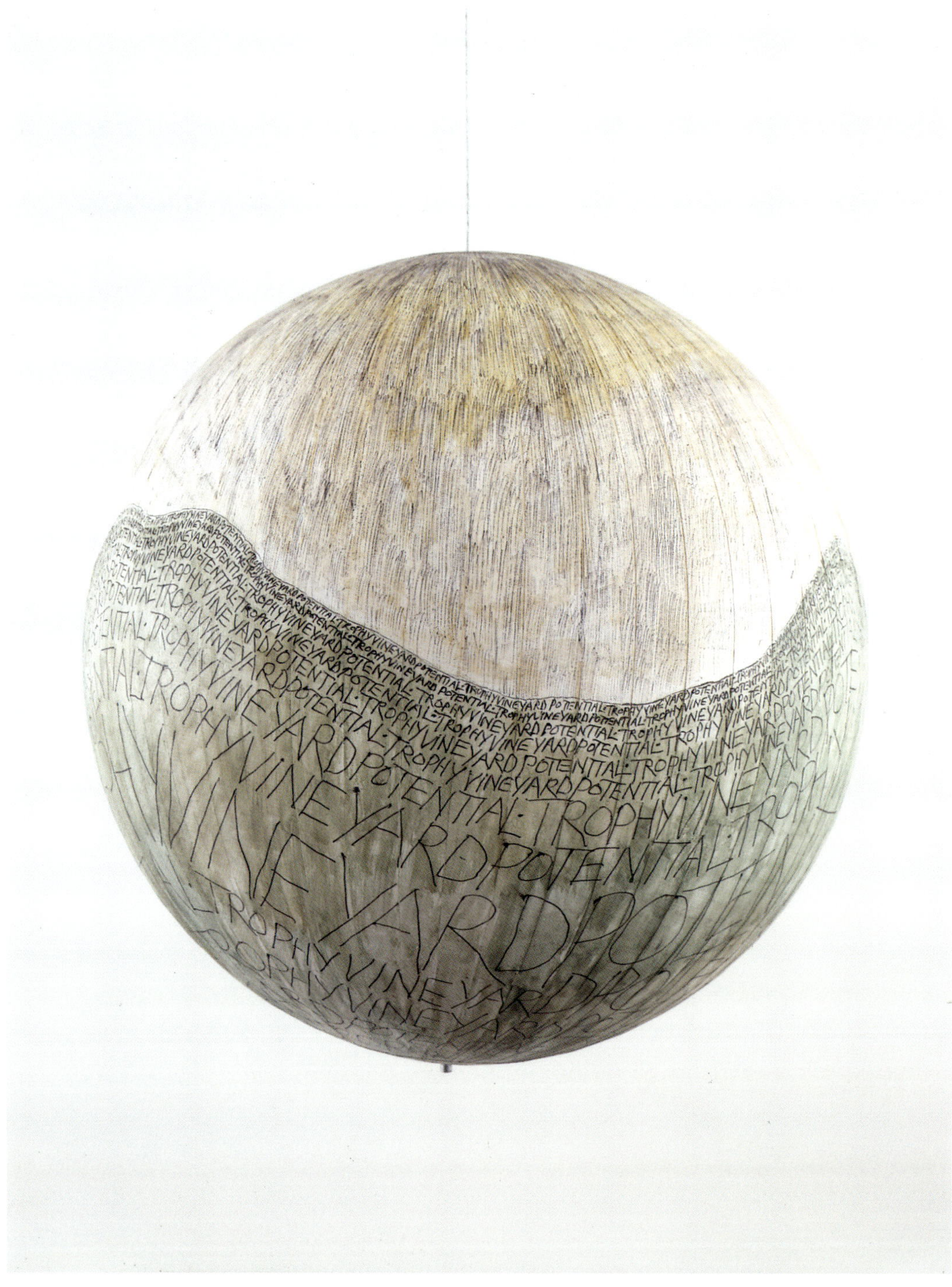

Russell Crotty, *Vineyard Potential*, ink and watercolor on paper mounted on fiberglass, 12 inch diameter. Courtesy of the Artist and CRG Gallery, New York.

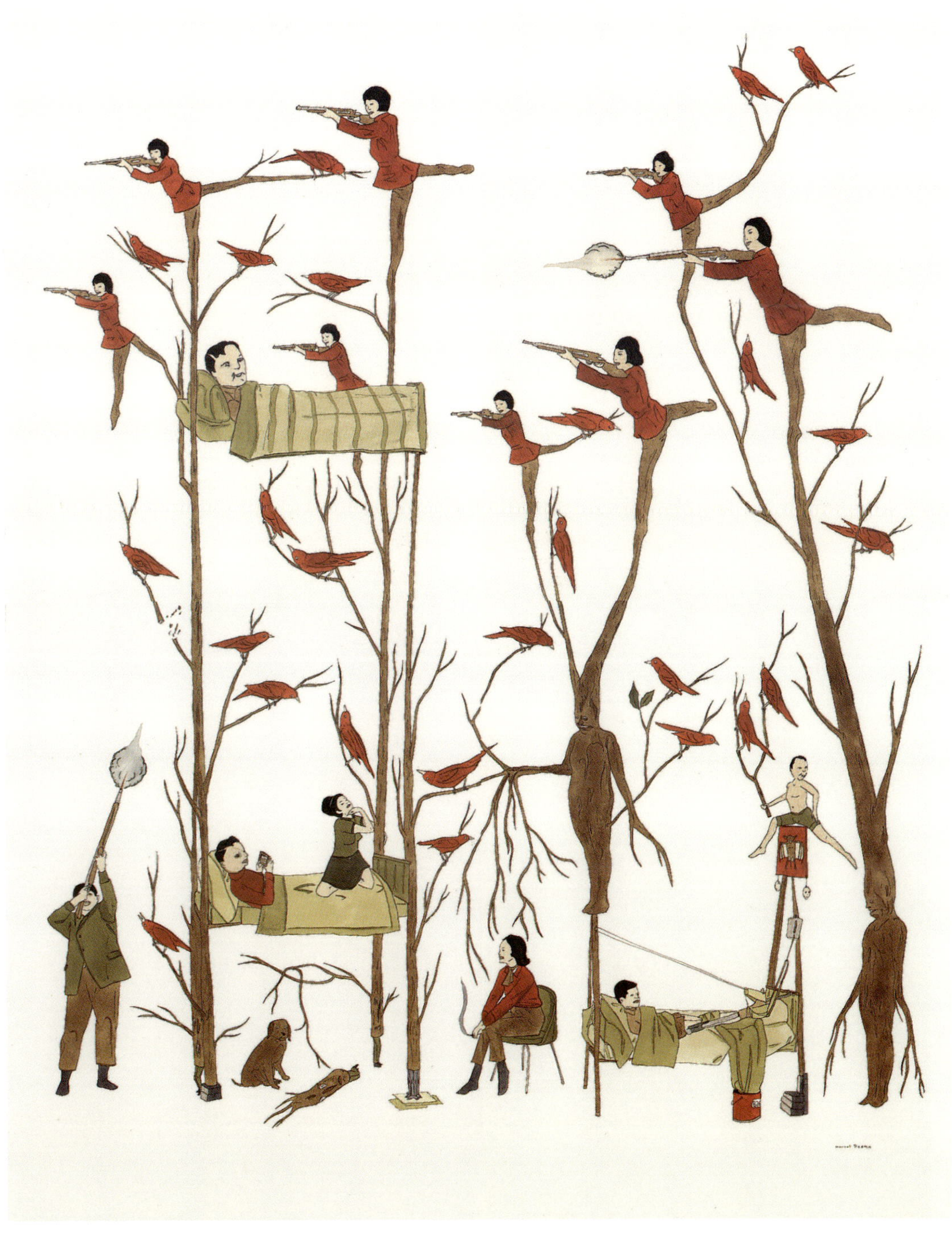

Marcel Dzama, *Eight Strong Winds*, 2005, ink and watercolor on paper, 4-part drawing, each drawing 14 x 11 inches, 28 x 22 inches overall. Private Collection, New York. Courtesy of David Zwirner, New York.

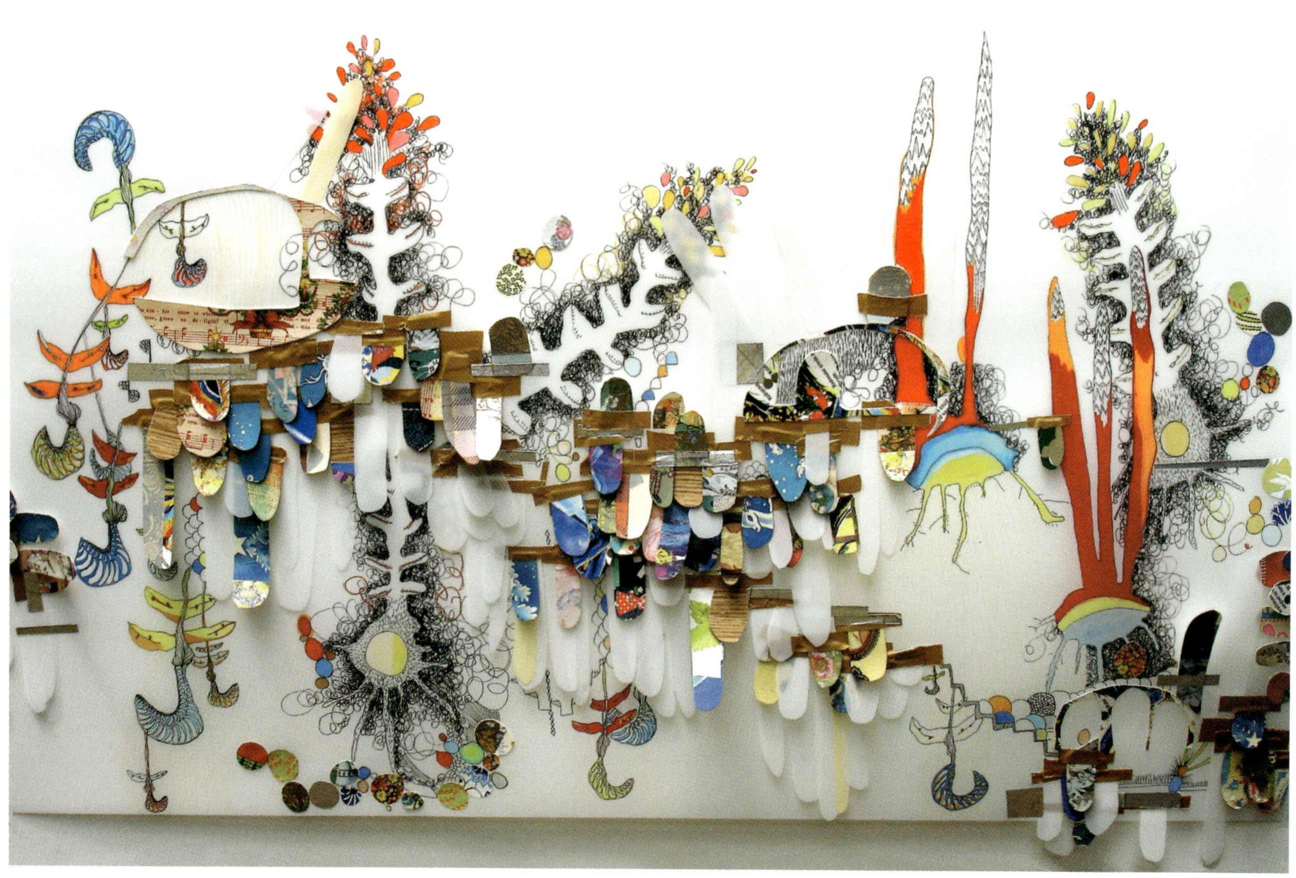

Janae Easton, *Robust Bark Encountered by Dusky Caves*, 2007, mylar, Lenox 100, wrapping paper, colored marker, colored pencil, pen, foil tape, duct tape, and other found papers, 25 x 40 inches.

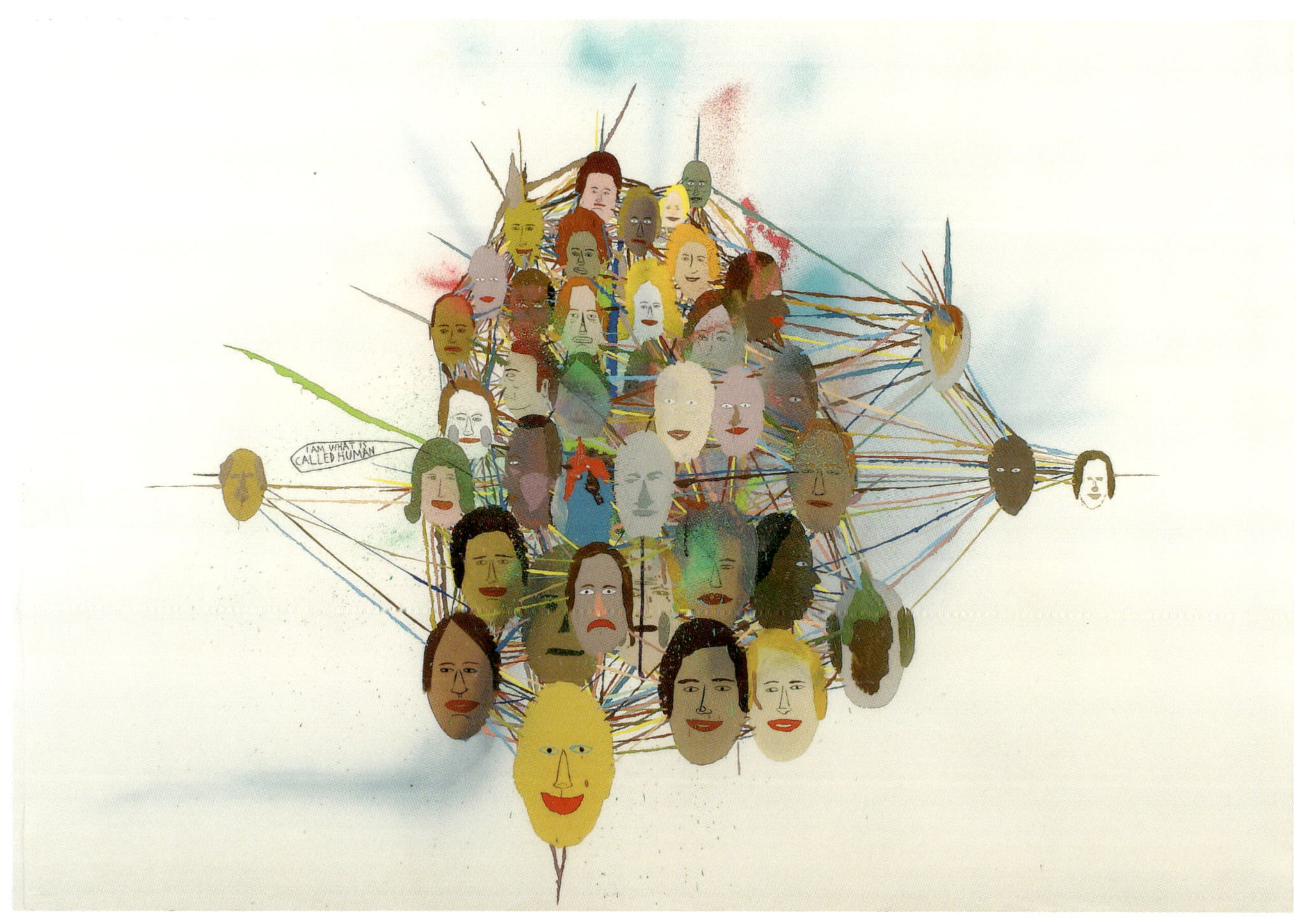


Chris Johanson, *Untitled (I am what is called human)*, 2005, acrylic on paper, 34 x 47 ¾ inches. Courtesy of the Artist and Kavi Gupta Gallery, Chicago.

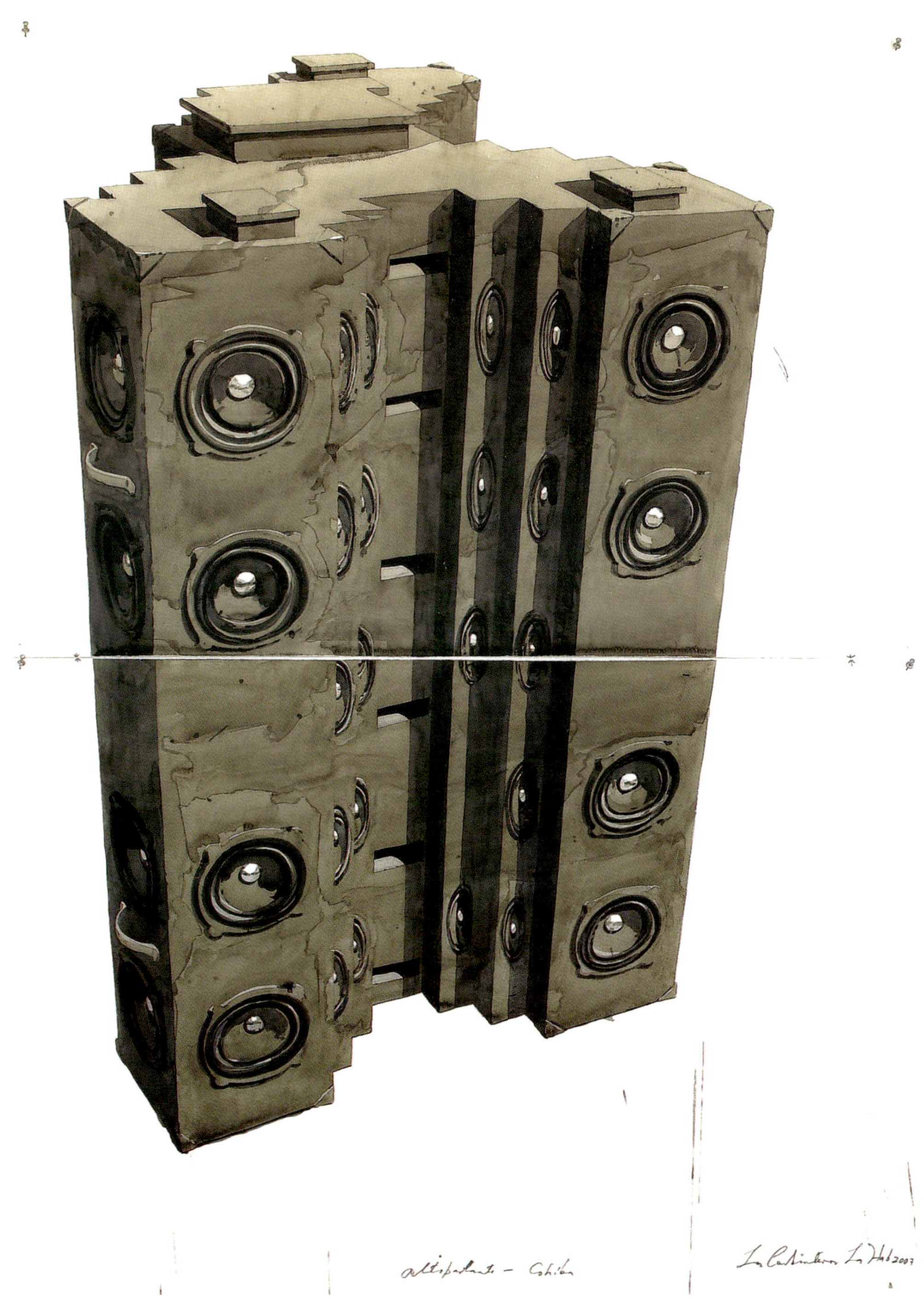

Los Carpinteros, *Alto Parlante—Cohiba* (diptych), 2007, watercolor on paper, 60 1/4 x 44 inches. Courtesy of Sean Kelly Gallery, New York.

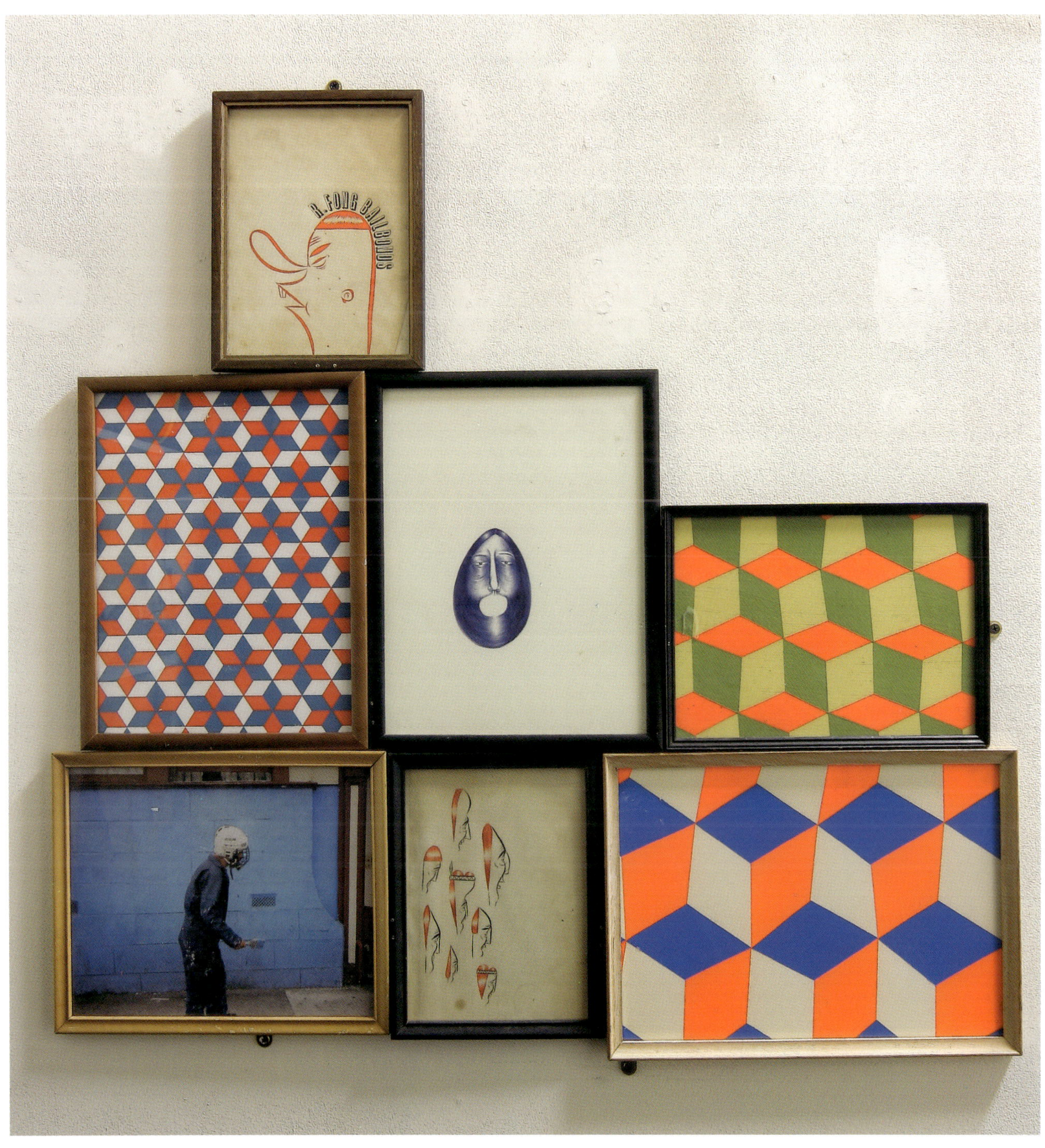

Barry McGee, *Grouping 2*, c. 2006, seven framed works on paper, 30 x 31 inches. Courtesy of the Artist and Gallery Paule Anglim, San Francisco.

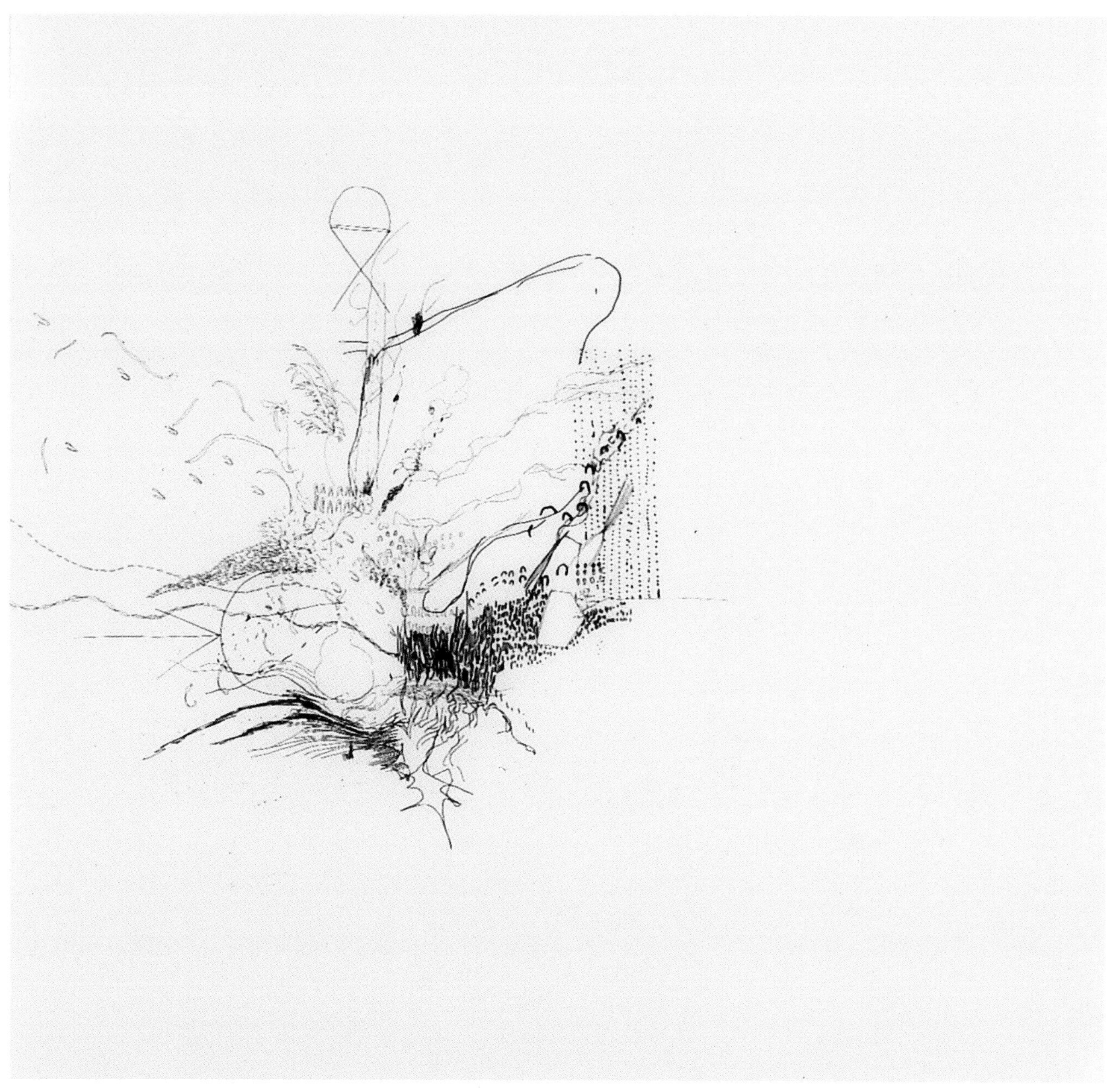

Julie Mehretu, *Untitled*, 2001, ink on mylar and paper, 19 x 20 inches. Collection of Christian Haye. Courtesy of The Project, New York.

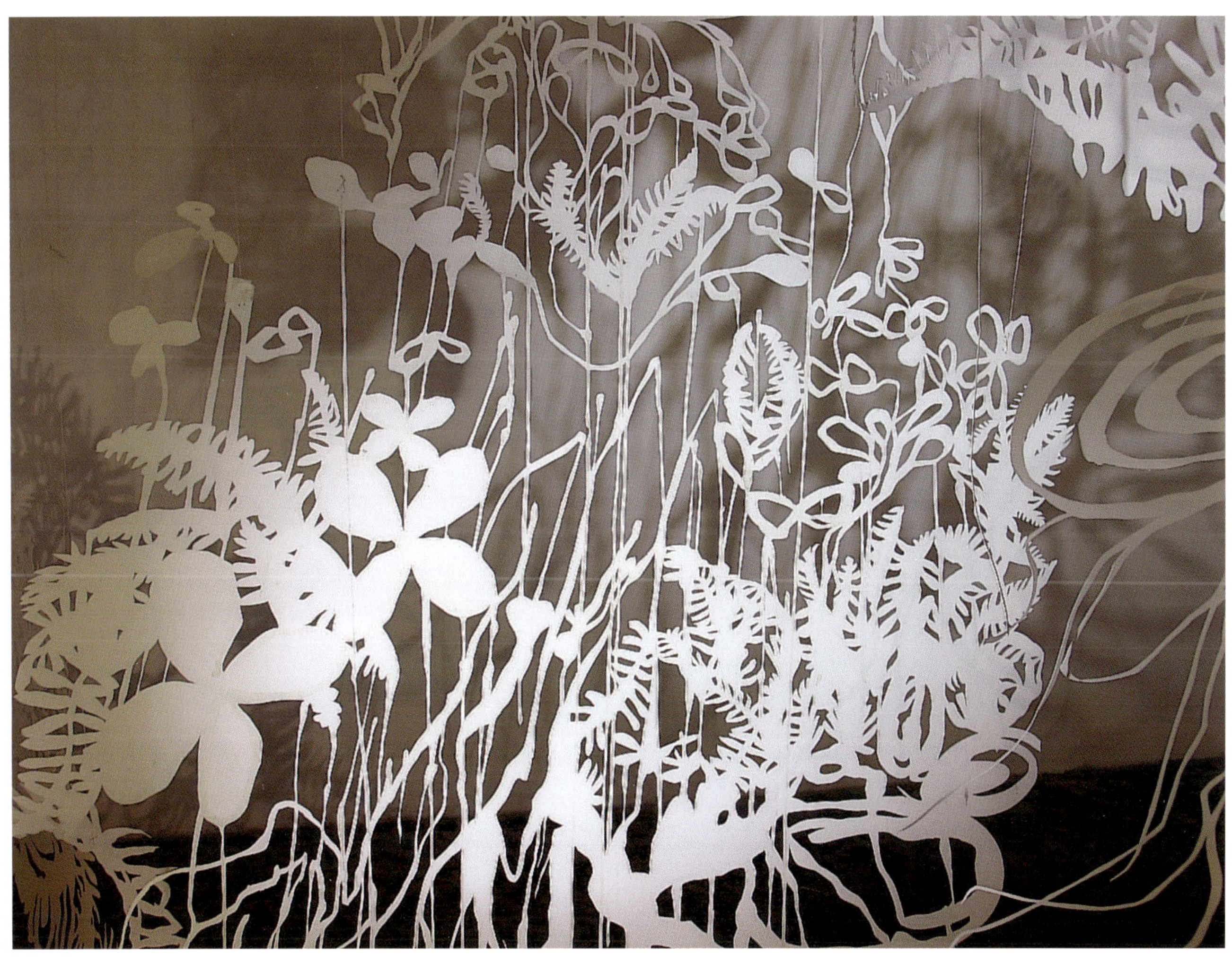

Chris Natrop, Detail of *Fern Space Burst*, 2004, hand cut paper, colored ink, watercolor, iridescent medium, tape, thread, 10 x 8 x 8 feet. Courtesy of the Artist.

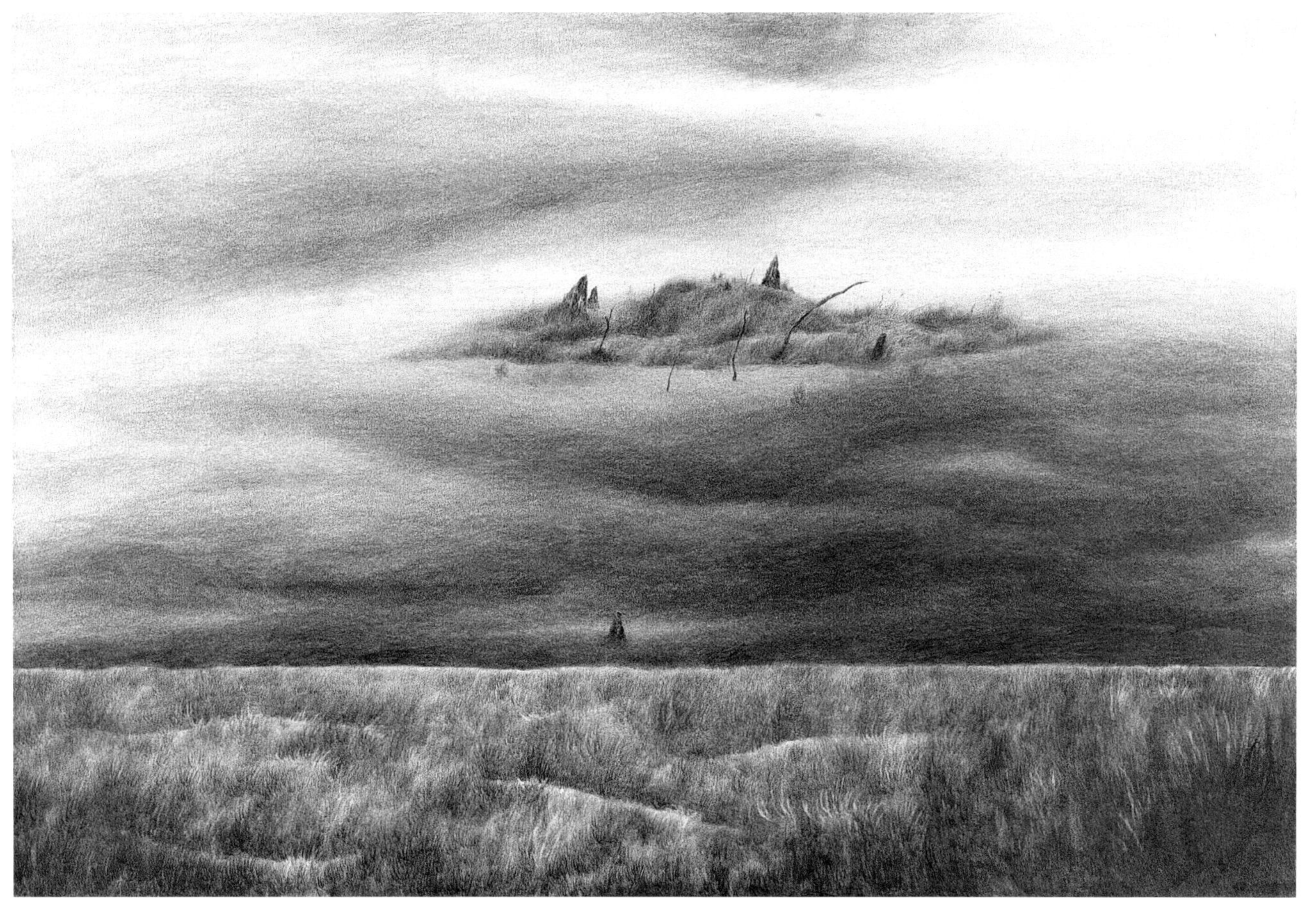

Robyn O'Neil, *This is a descending world*, 2007, graphite on paper, 14 x 22 inches. Courtesy of the Artist and Clementine Gallery, New York.

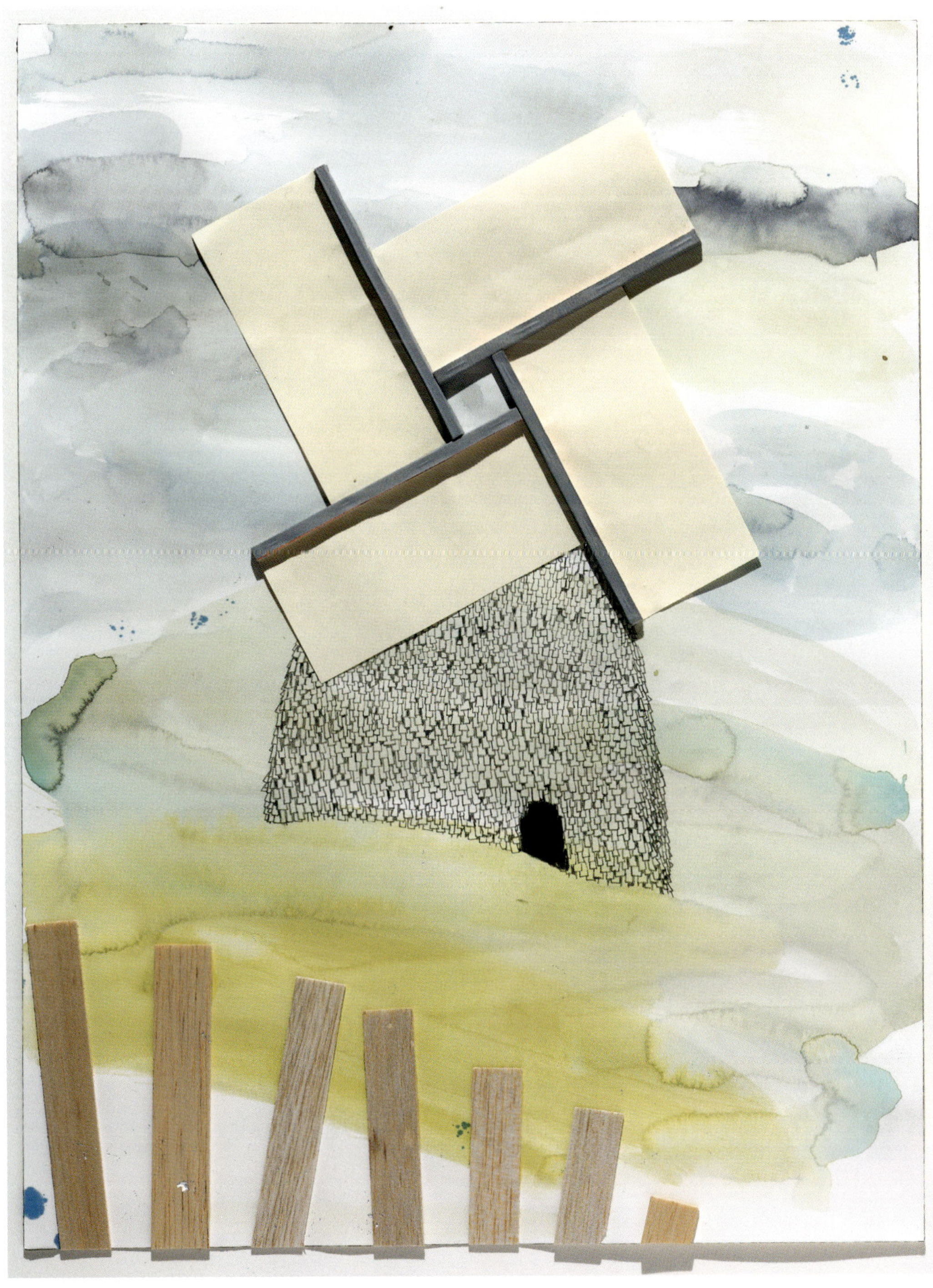

Laura Owens, *Untitled*, 2003, acrylic, pencil and collage on paper, 24 x 18 inches. Collection of Matt Aberle, Los Angeles. Courtesy of the Artist and Gavin Brown's enterprise, New York.

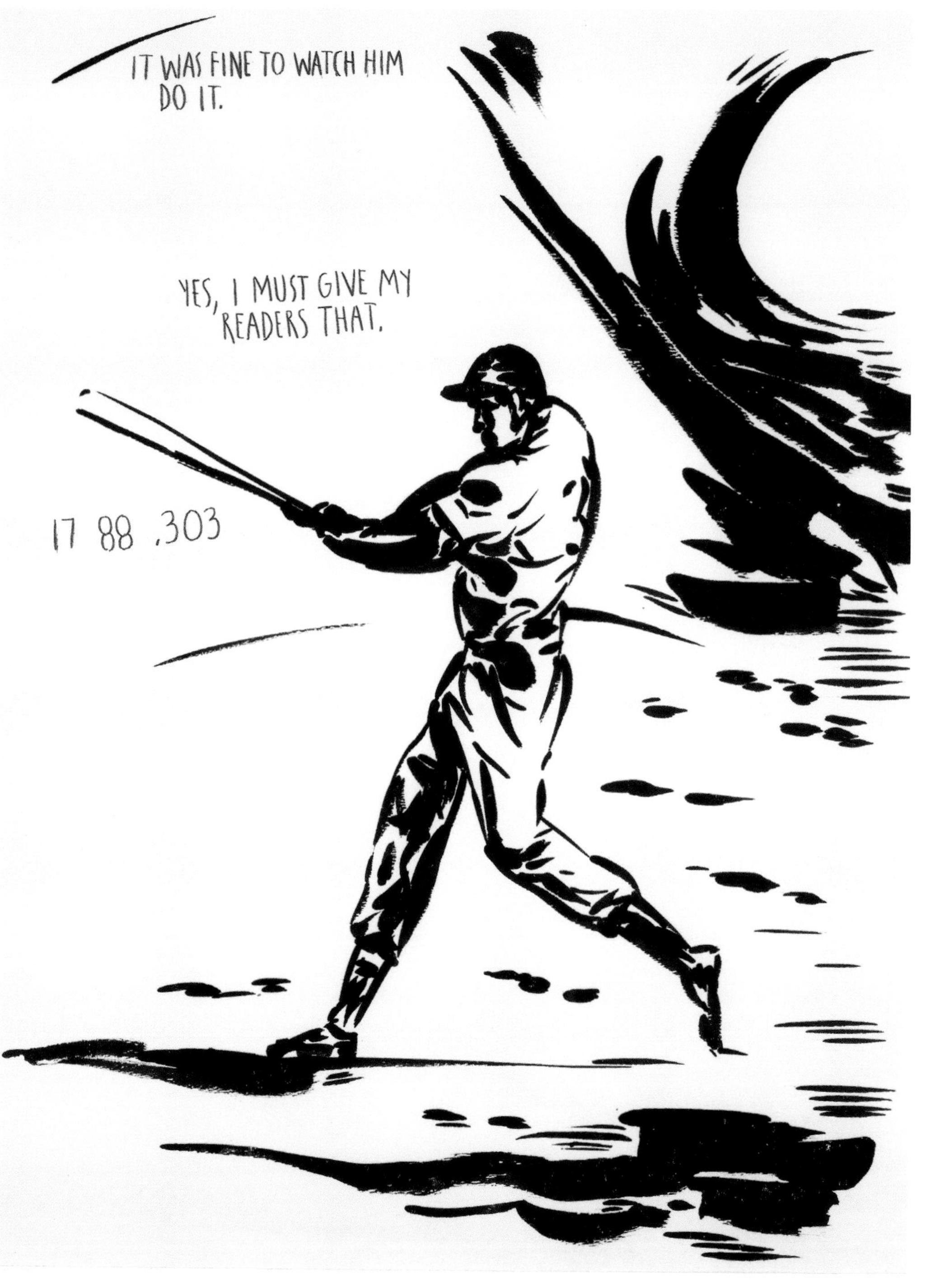



Raymond Pettibon, *Untitled (It was fine…)*, 1991, ink on paper, 24 ½ x 18 inches. Courtesy of the Artist and Rita Krauss Fine Art / Meridian Gallery, New York. Photo credit: Jon Nalon.

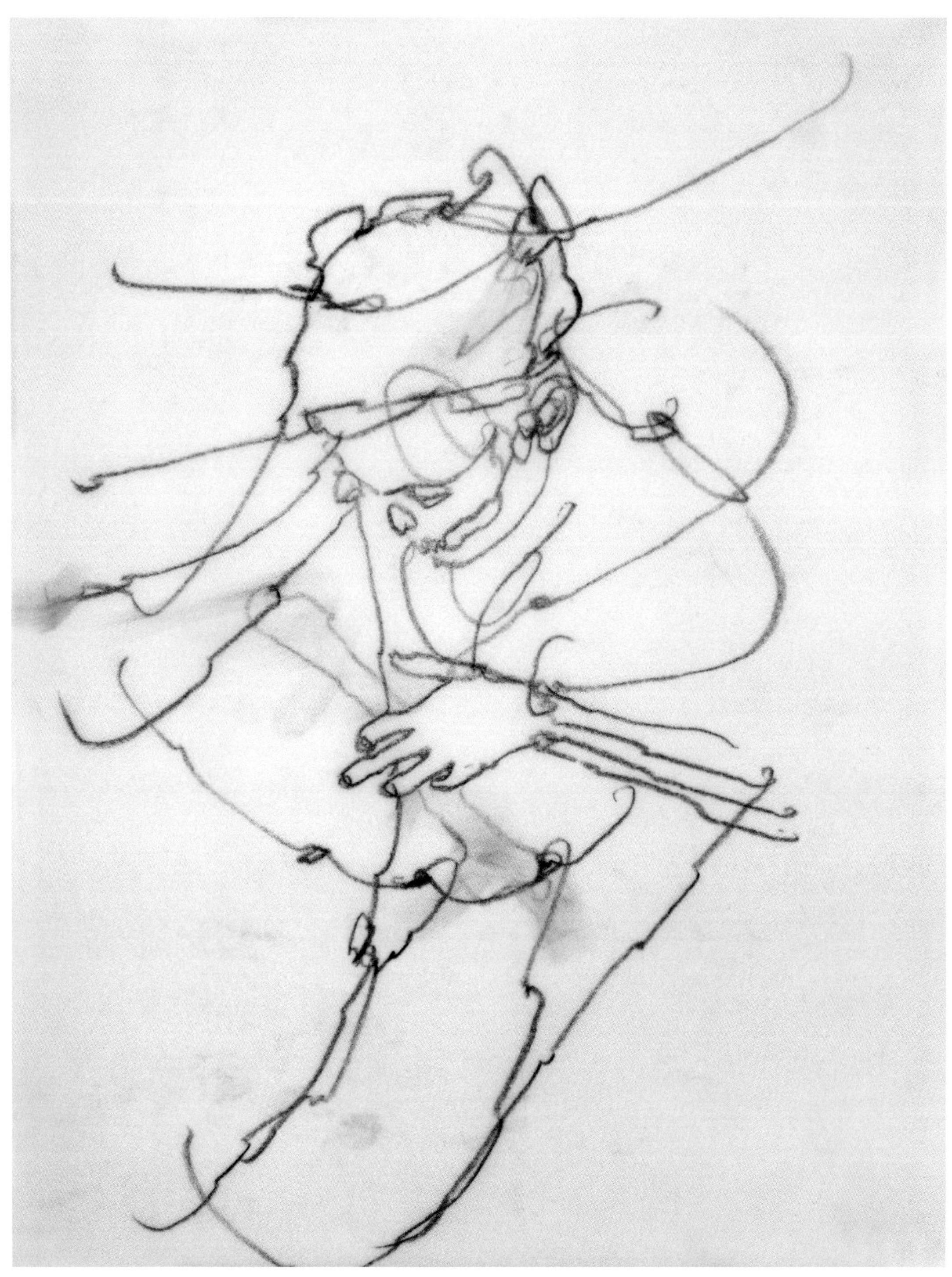

Chloe Piene, *Careful Hand*, 2007, charcoal on vellum, 12 x 9 inches. Courtesy of the Artist and SandroniRey, Los Angeles.

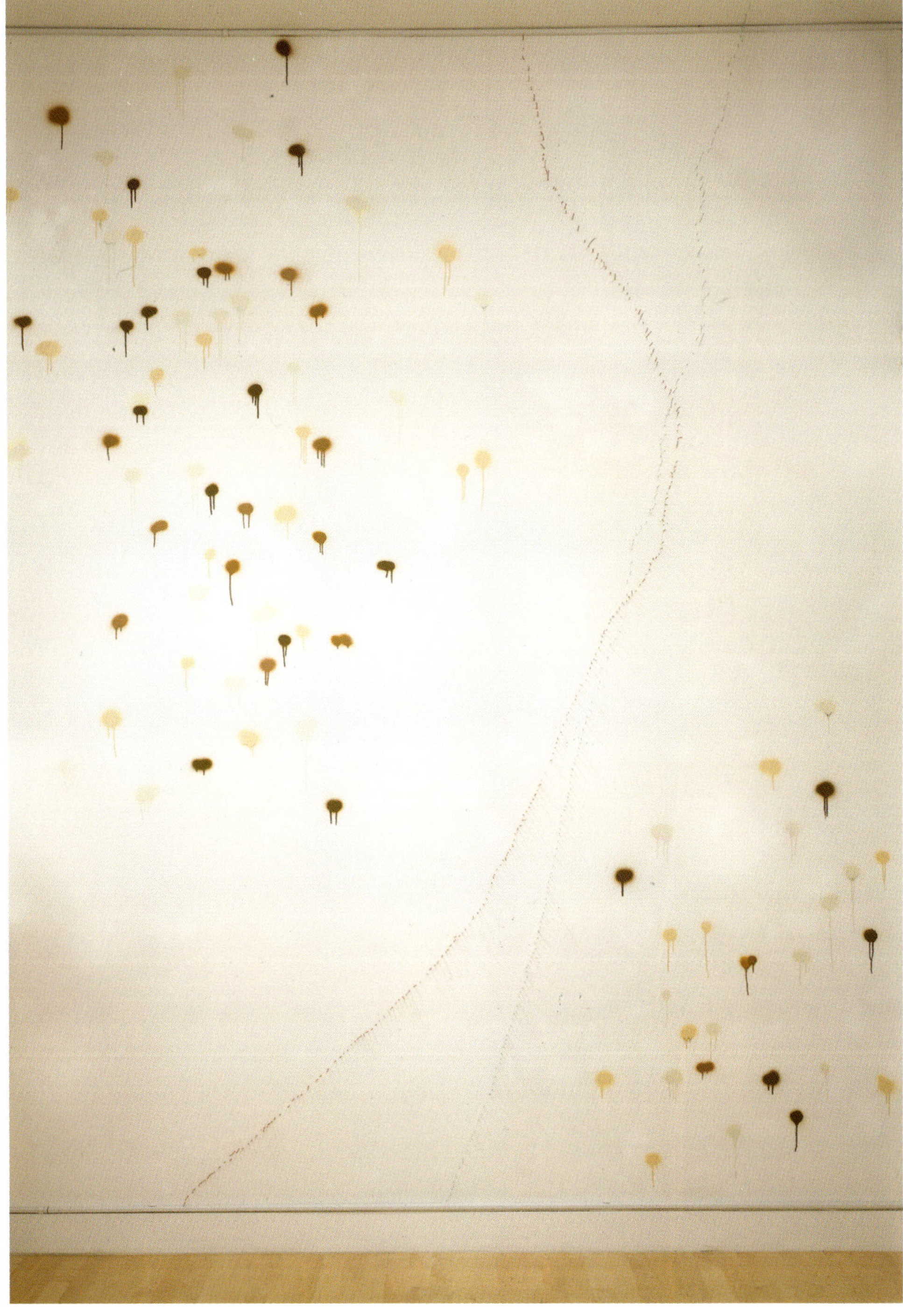

Amy Rathbone, *Plebians*, 2004, spray enamel, wire and pencil on wall, dimensions variable. Courtesy of the Artist and Gregory Lind Gallery, San Francisco.

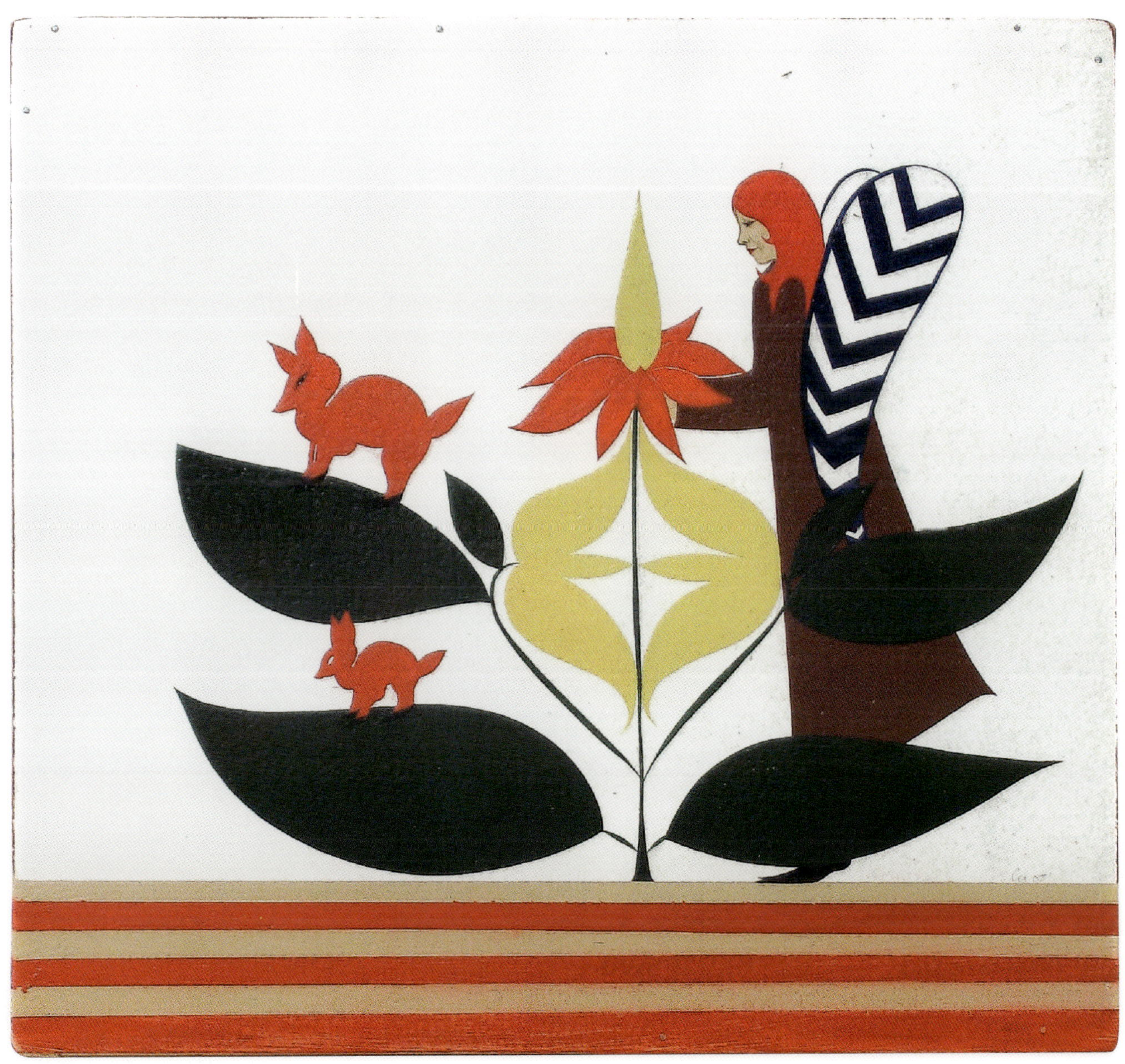

Clare Rojas, *Untitled (woman holding flower)*, 2007, gouache and latex on panel, 12 x 12 inches. Courtesy of the Artist and Gallery Paule Anglim, San Francisco.

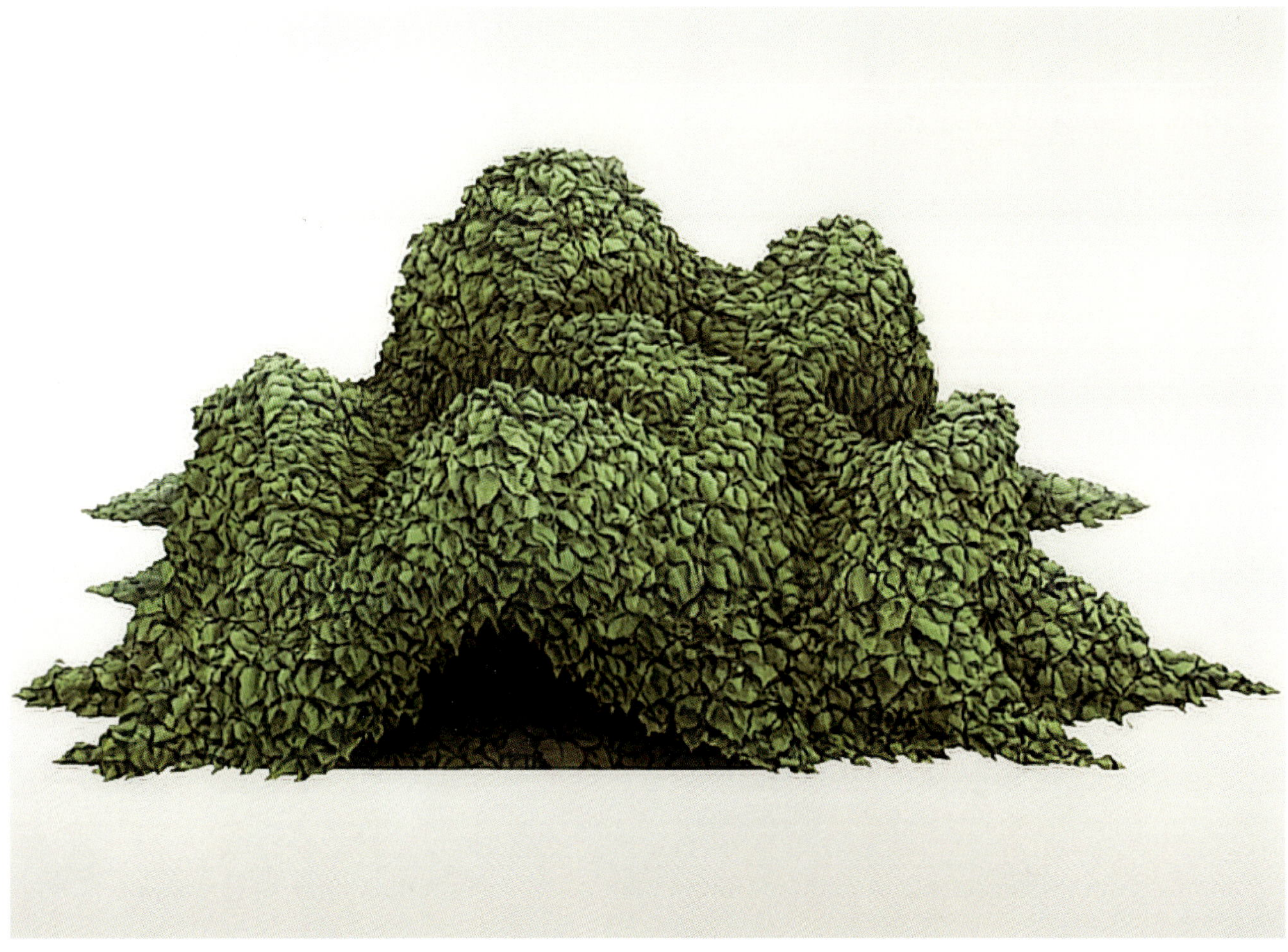

Gina Ruggeri, *Overgrowth*, 2005, acrylic on mylar, 42 x 87 inches. Courtesy of the Artist and Kevin Bruk Gallery, Miami.

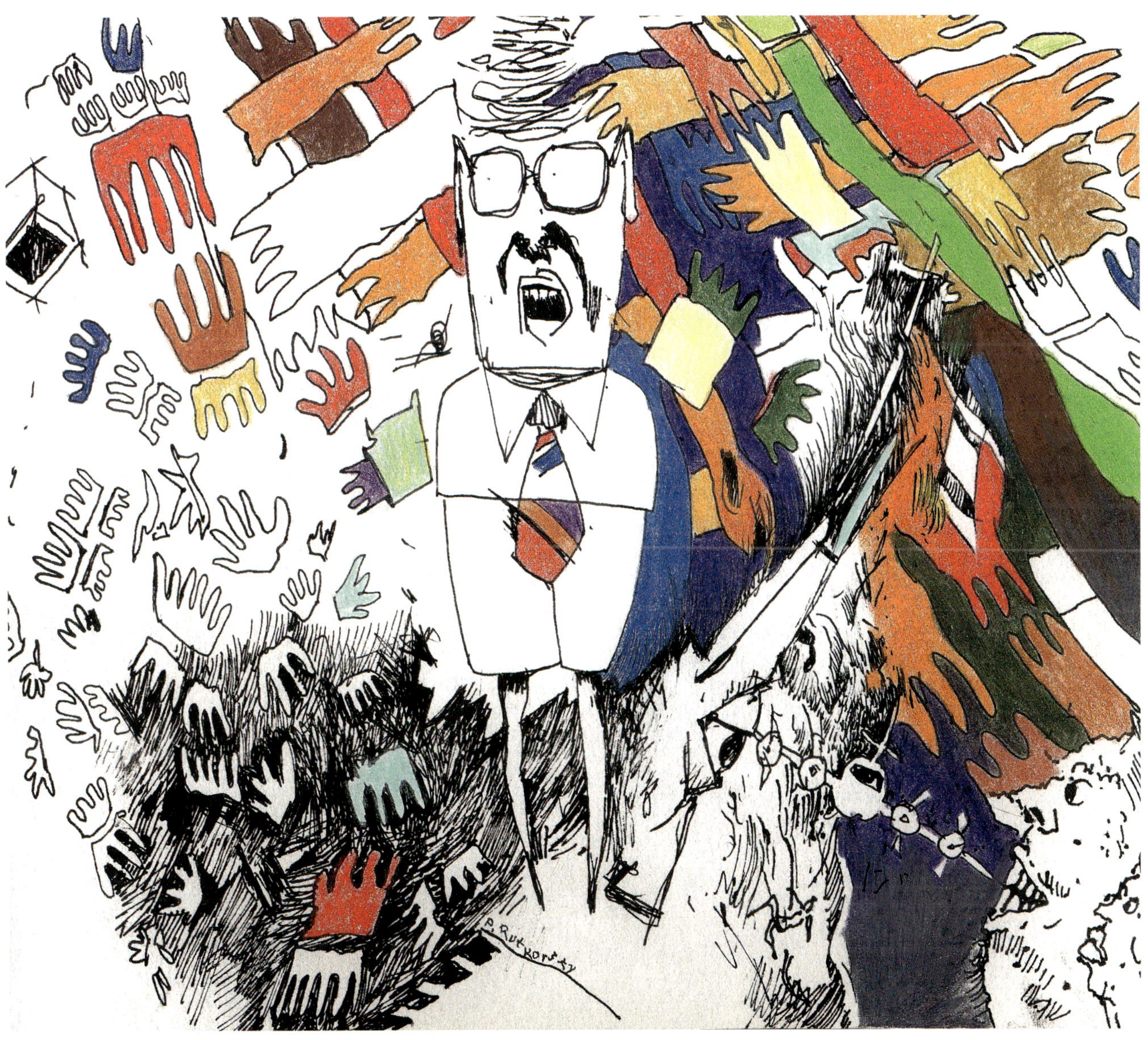

Paul Rutkovsky, *Merry to the End*, 2005, pen and ink, colored pencil, 7 x 8 inches. Courtesy of the Artist.

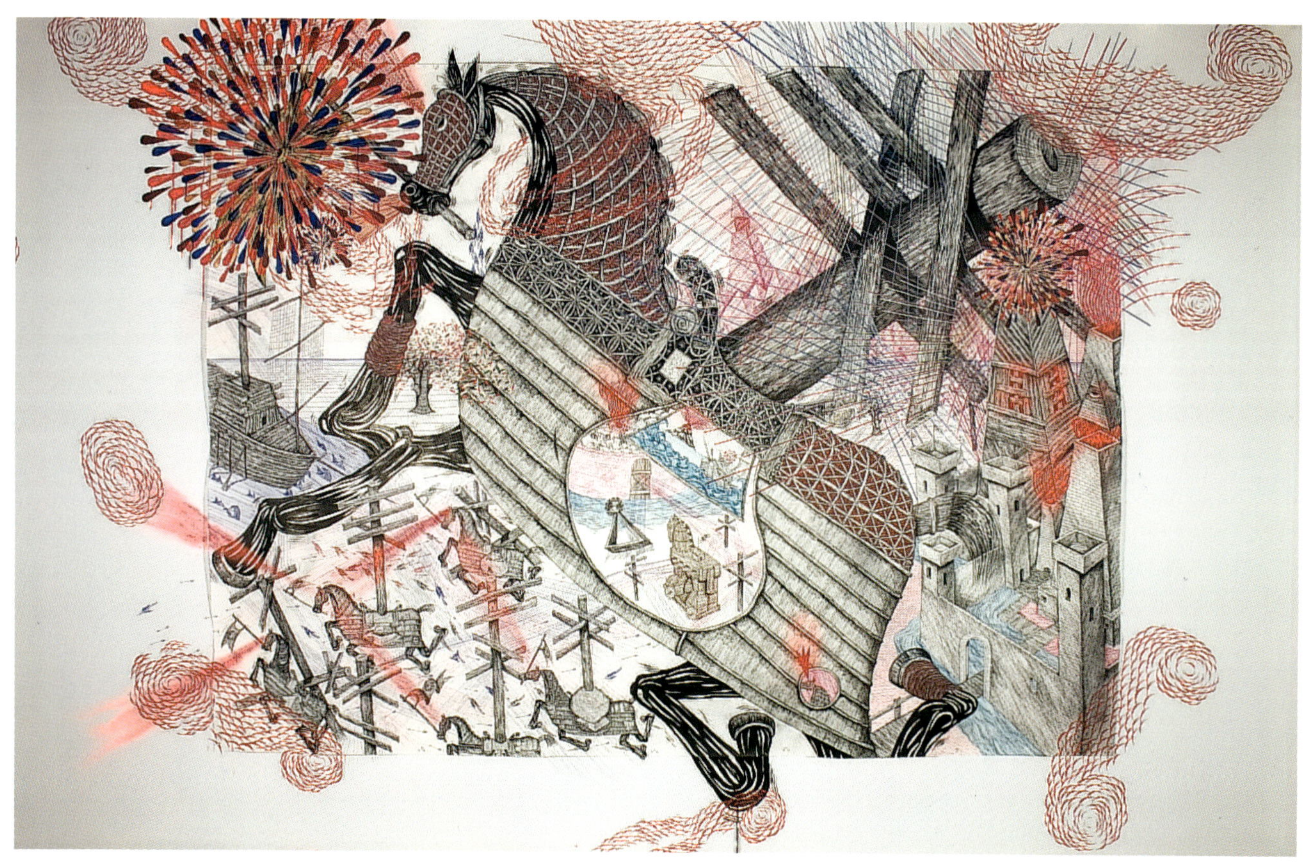

Andrew Schoultz, *Trampled Under Hoof*, 2007, mixed media on paper, 7 x 9 feet. Courtesy of Morgan Lehman Gallery, New York, and Heather Marx Gallery, San Francisco.

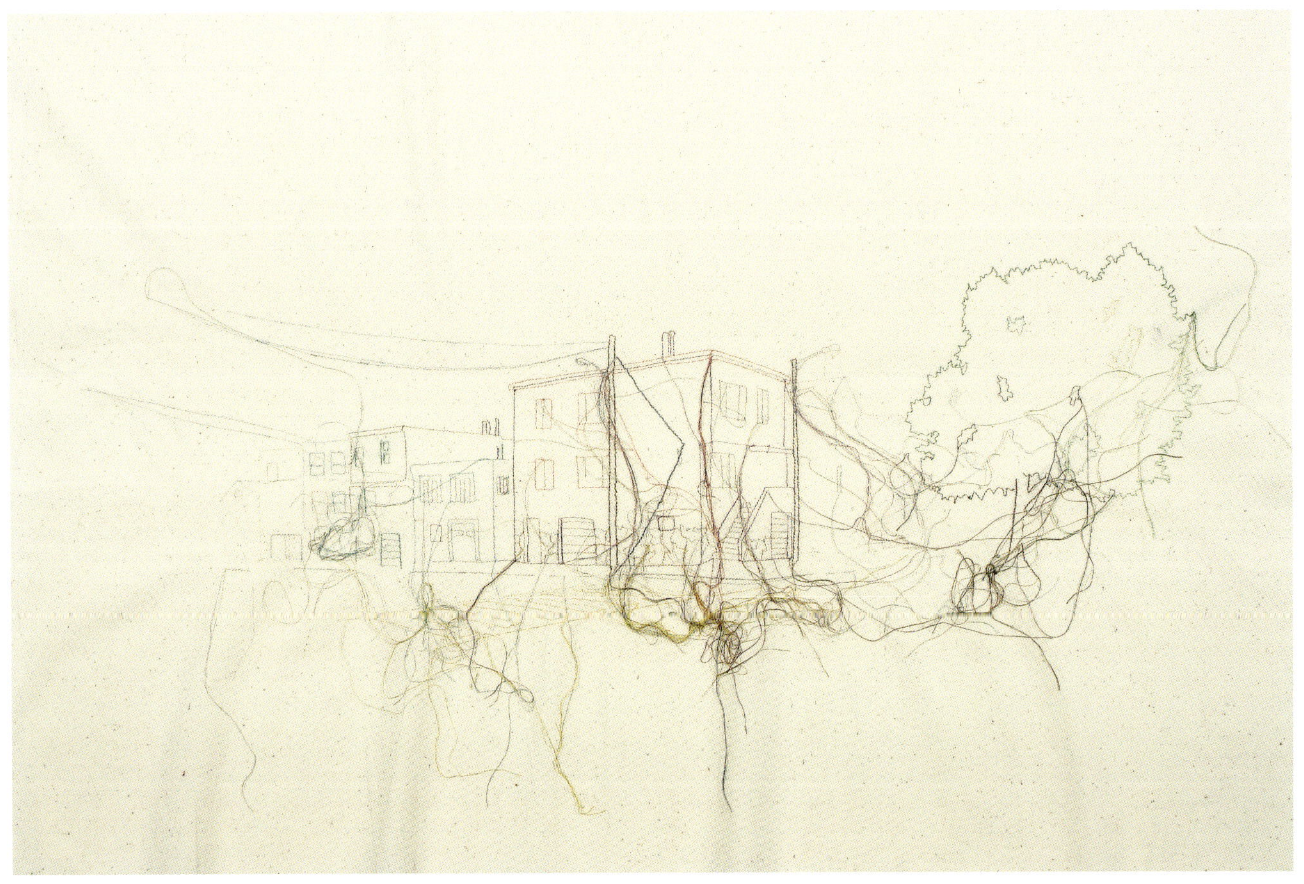

Tucker Schwarz, *Nothing can save me now*, 2005, thread on muslin, 30 x 49 inches. Courtesy of the Artist and Gregory Lind Gallery, San Francisco.

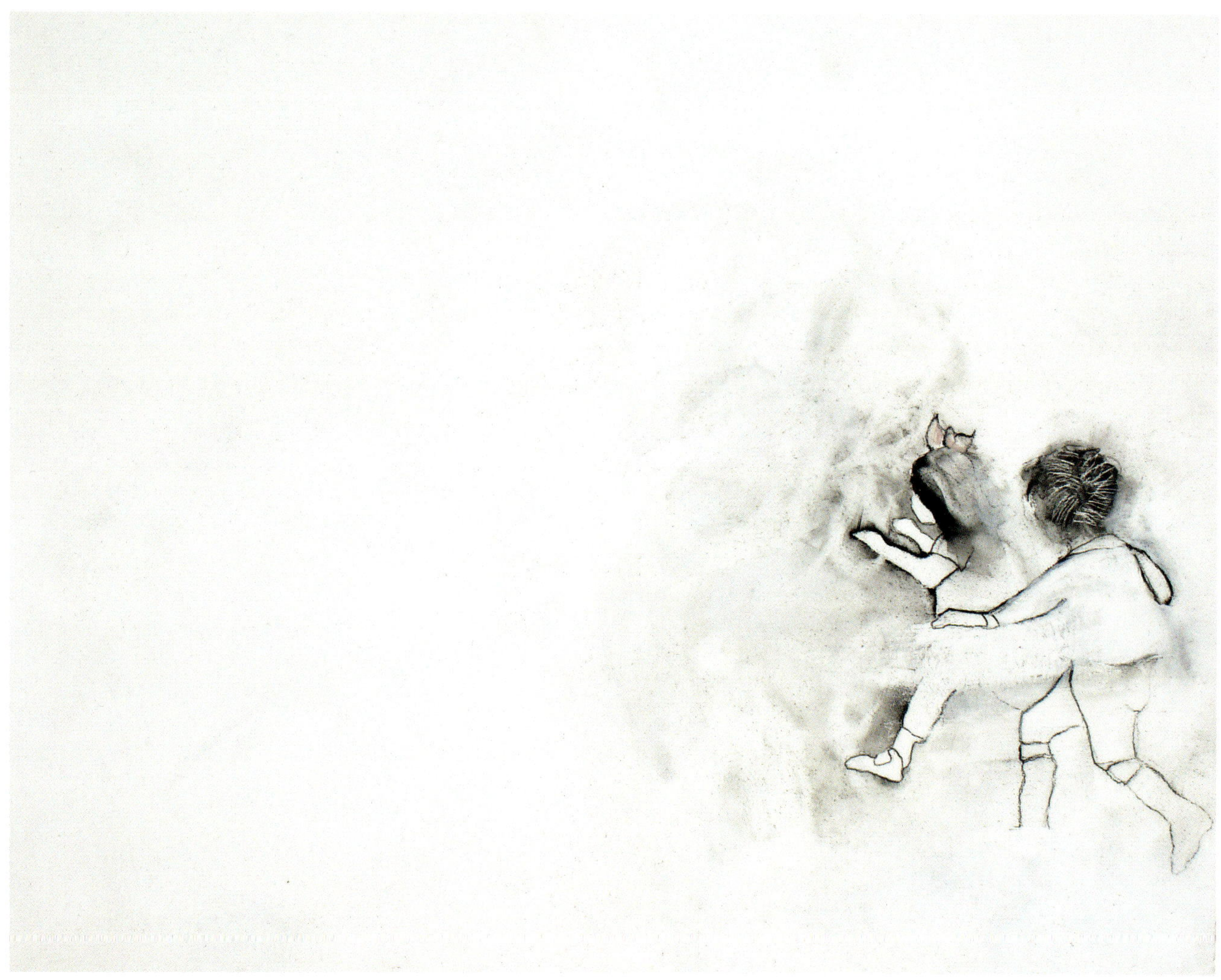

Kirsten Rae Simonsen, *Running Scared*, 2007, charcoal, pencil, acrylic, and gesso on wood panel, 11 x 14 inches. Courtesy of the Artist.

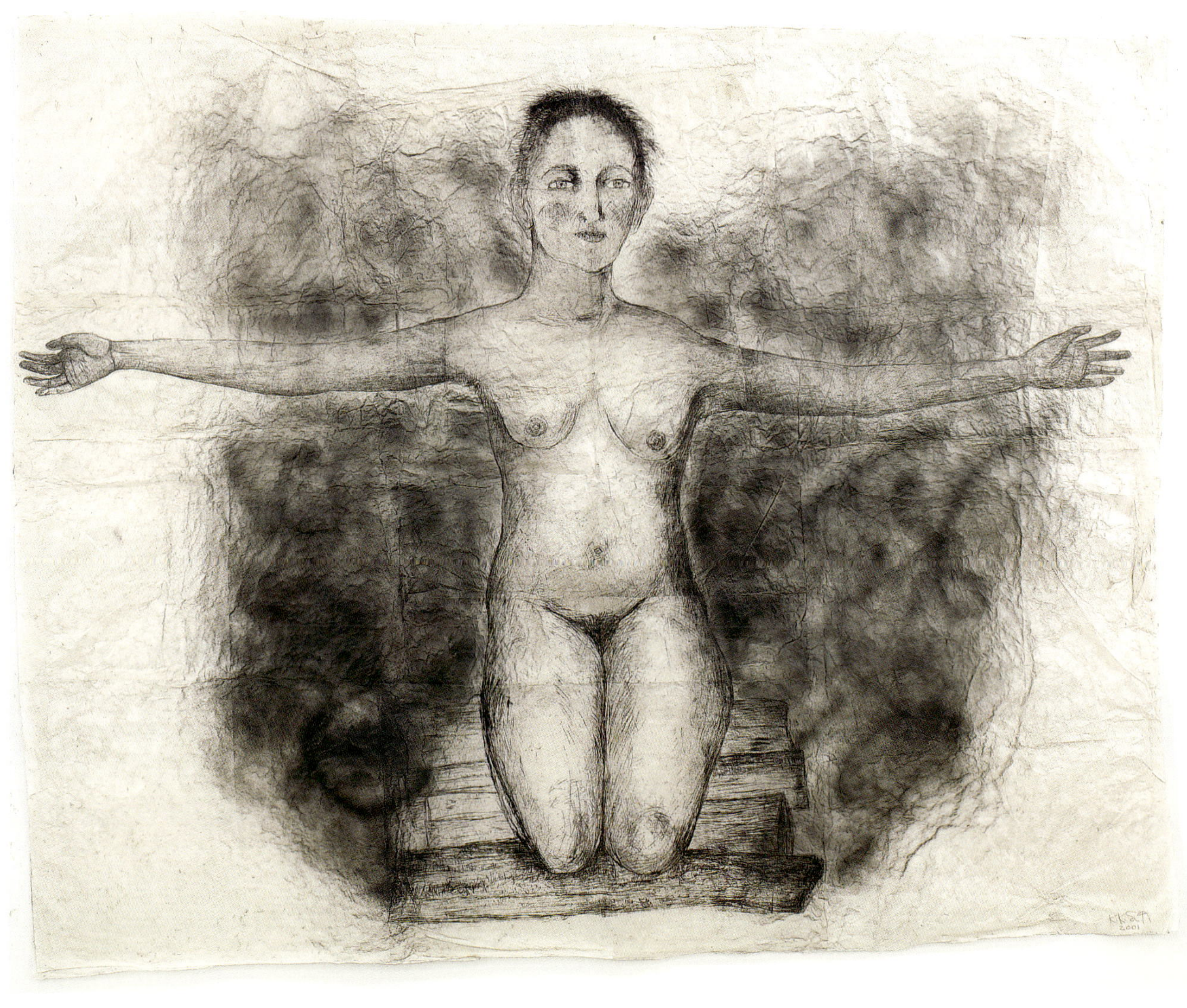

Kiki Smith, *Woman on Pyre*, 2001, ink on Nepal paper, 61 x 75.5 inches; Pyre, 2001, ink on Nepal paper, 77.5 x 70 inches. Courtesy of the Artist and PaceWildenstein, New York.

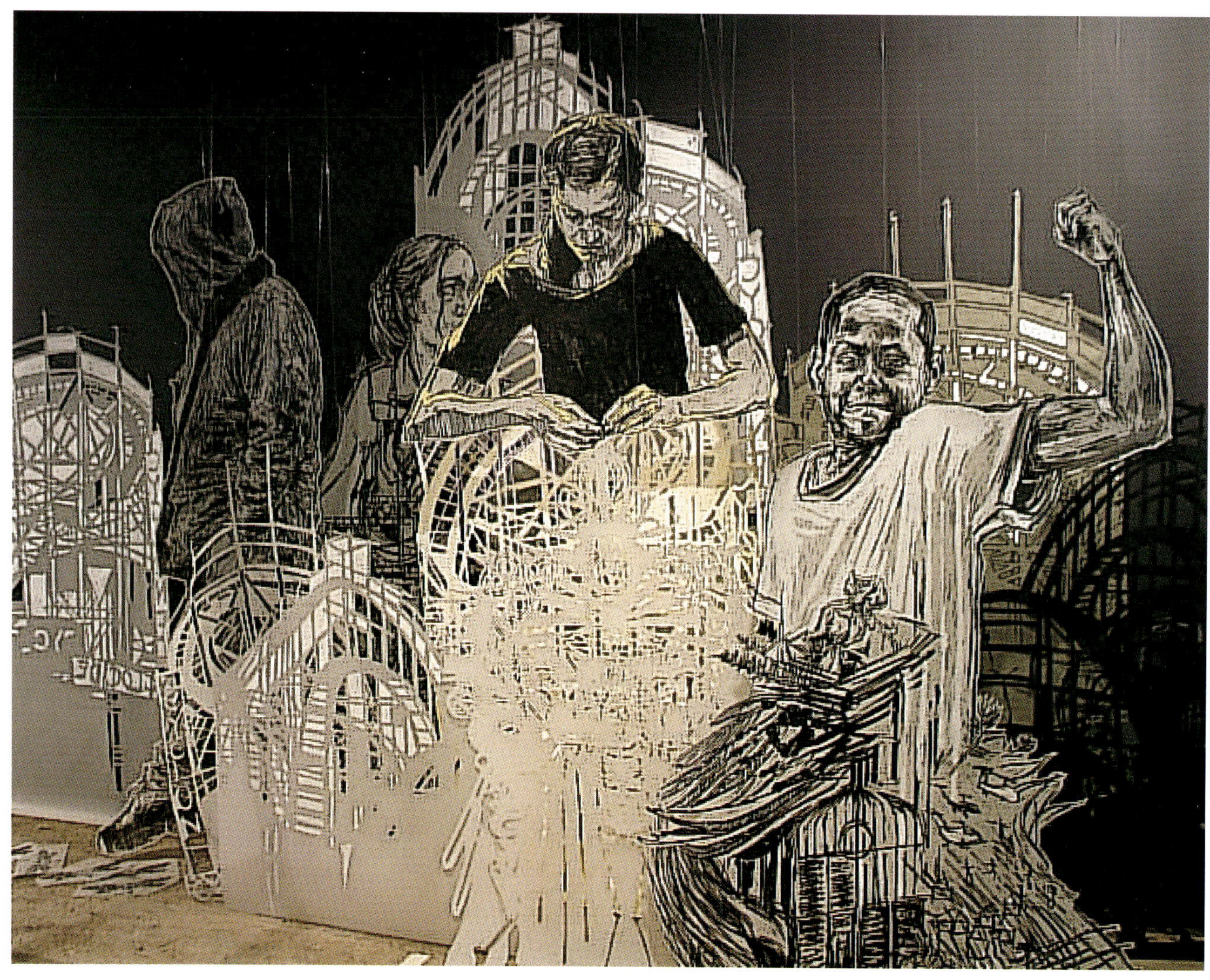

Swoon, *Untitled*, 2005, mixed media, dimensions variable. Collection of the Brooklyn Museum of Art, courtesy of Deitch Projects, New York.

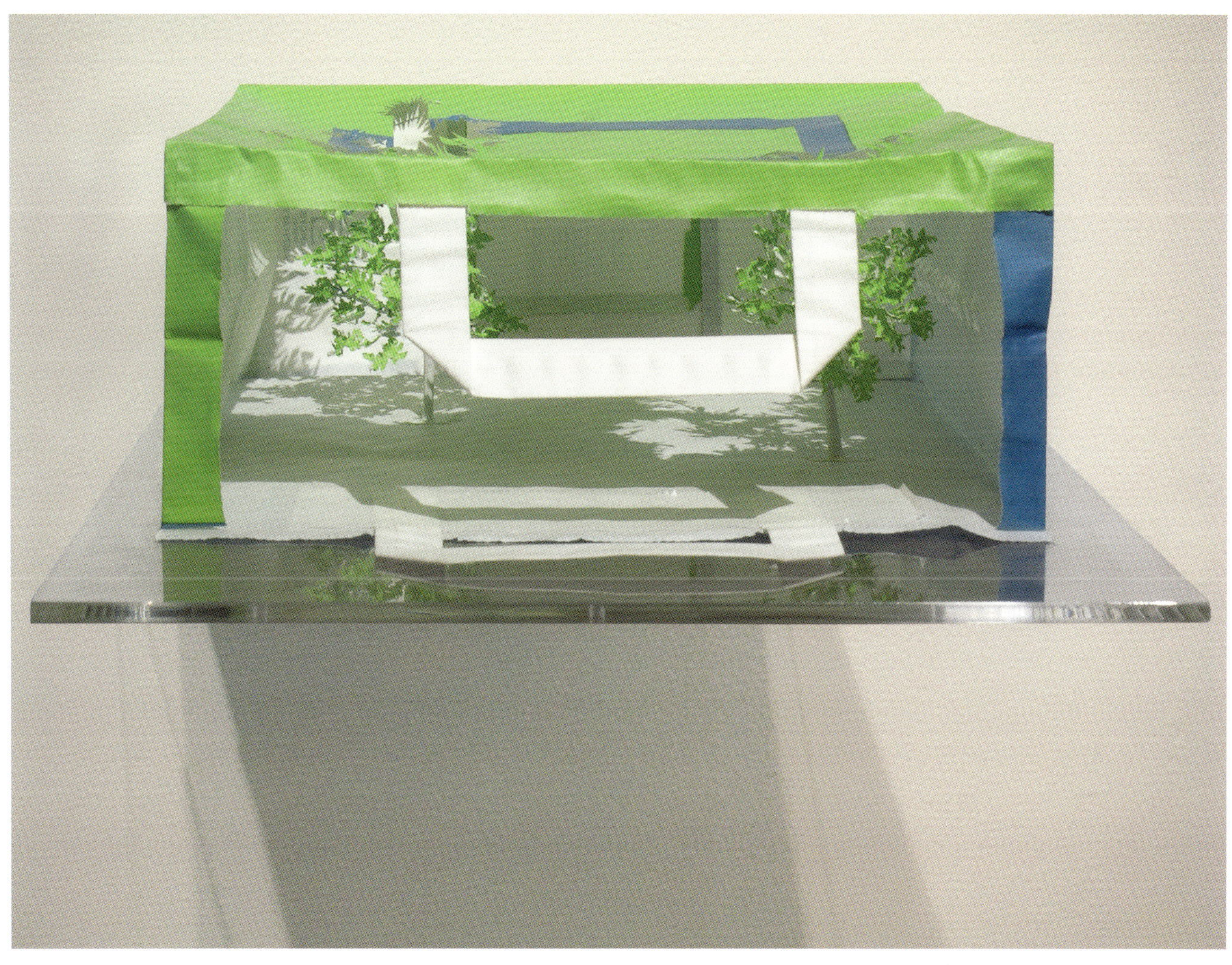

Yuken Teruya, *Notice Forest (Graz Zweitausenddrei)*, 2006, paper bag, 4 ½ x 9 ¾ x 16 inches. Courtesy of the Artist and Shoshana Wayne Gallery, Santa Monica.

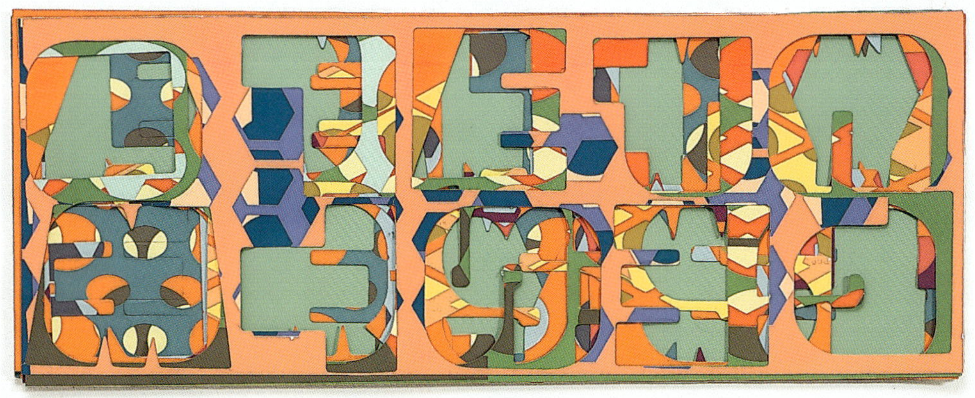

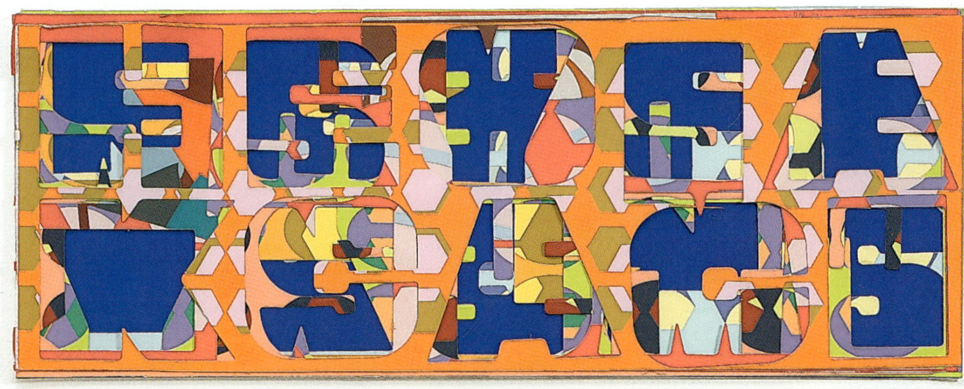

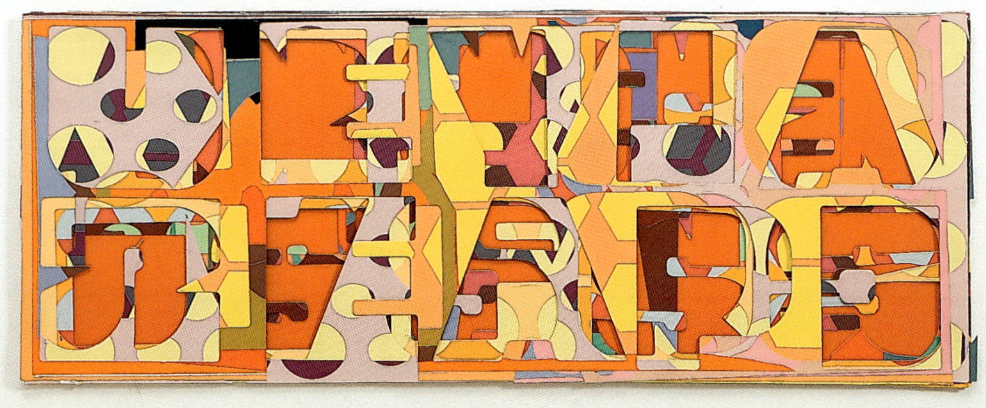

Pae White, *Noisy Letters (Blue)*, *Noisy Letters (Green)*, *Noisy Letters (Yellow)*, 2006, collage, 37 x 25 inches. Courtesy of the Artist and 1301PE, Los Angeles. Photo credit: Fredrik Nilsen.

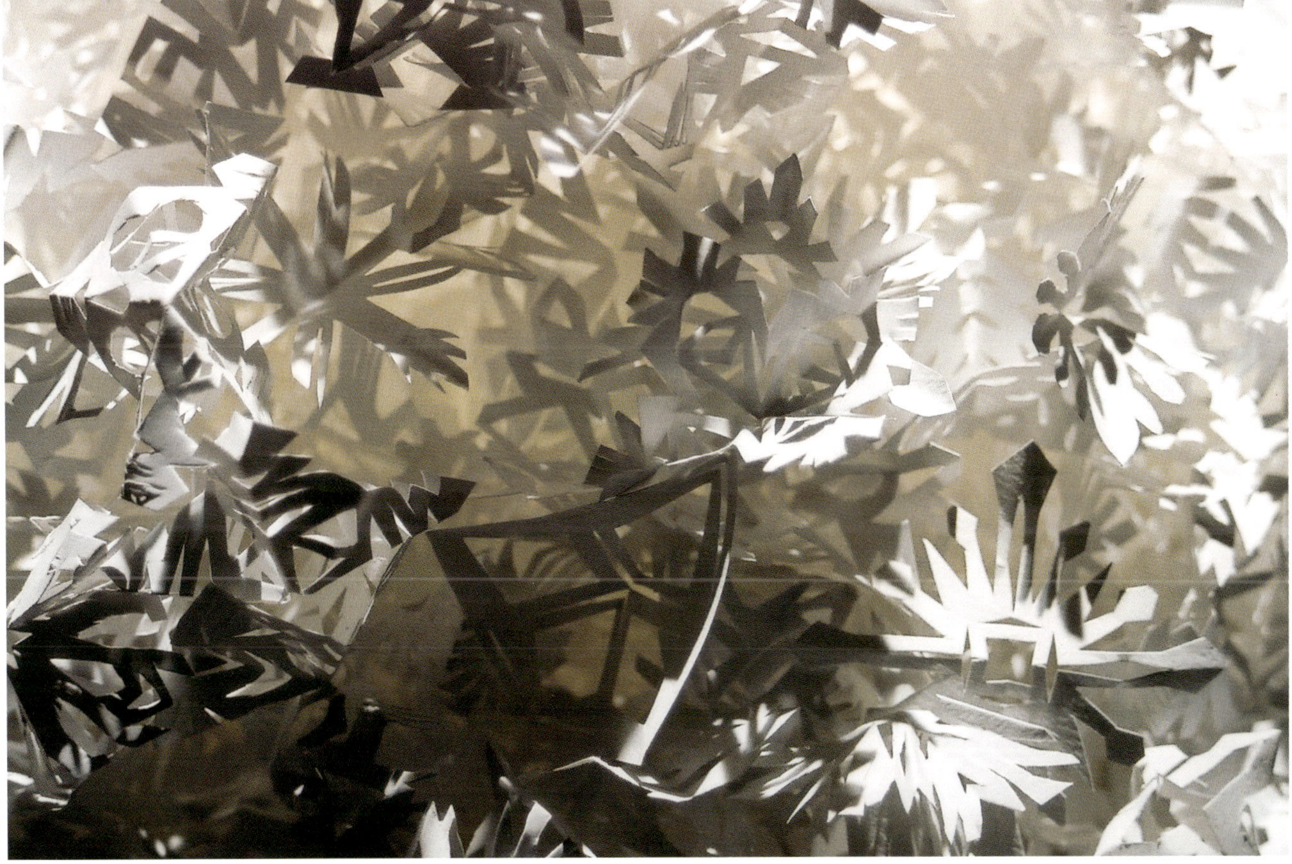

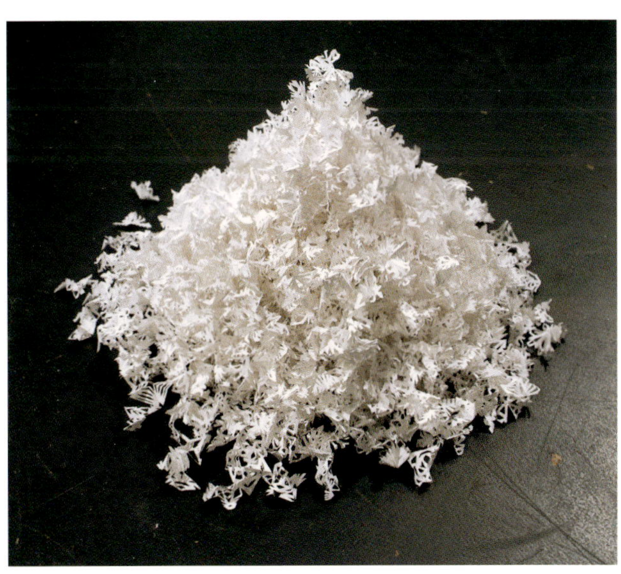

Wendy Wischer, Detail of *Longing* and installation, 2004, cut paper, 18 x 16 inches diameter. Courtesy of the Artist and David Castillo Gallery, Miami.

- Laylah Ali, *Untitled* (LA 134), 2004, ink on paper, 9 ½ x 7 ½ inches; *Untitled* (LA 136), 2004, ink on paper, 9 ½ x 7 ½ inches; *Untitled* (LA 138), 2004, ink on paper, 9 ½ x 7 ½ inches. Courtesy of the Artist and 303 Gallery, New York.

- Louis Bourgeois, *Untitled*, 1971, ink on lined paper, 8 x 5 ¾ inches. Courtesy of the Artist and Cheim & Read, New York.

- Russell Crotty, *Vineyard Potential*, ink and watercolor on paper mounted on fiberglass, 12 inch diameter. Courtesy of the Artist and CRG Gallery, New York.

- Marcel Dzama, *Eight Strong Winds*, 2005 ink and watercolor on paper, 4-part drawing, each drawing 14 x 11 inches, 28 x 22 inches overall. Private Collection, New York. Courtesy of David Zwirner, New York.

- Janae Easton, *Robust Bark Encountered by Dusky Caves*, 2007, mylar, Lenox 100, wrapping paper, colored marker, colored pencil, pen, foil tape, duct tape, and other found papers, 25 x 40 inches.

- Chris Johanson, *Untitled (I am what is called human)*, 2005, acrylic on paper, 34 x 47 ¾ inches. Courtesy of the Artist and Kavi Gupta Gallery, Chicago.

- Los Carpinteros, *Pool-Pool (Estudio Final)*, 2006, watercolor on paper, diptych, 29 x 85 inches framed. Collection of Nedra and Mark Oren. Courtesy of Sean Kelly Gallery, New York.

- Barry McGee, *Grouping 2*, c. 2006, seven framed works on paper, 30 x 31 inches. Courtesy of the Artist and Gallery Paule Anglim, San Francisco; *Untitled*, 1998, pencil and marker on paper, 9 7/8 x 8 inches. Courtesy of the Artist and Paul Morris Gallery, New York.

- Julie Mehretu, *Untitled* (JM-D-37.01), 2001, ink on mylar and paper, 19 x 20 inches; *Untitled*(JM-D-52.01), 2001, ink on mylar and paper, 19 x 20 inches. Collection of Christian Haye. Courtesy of the Artist and The Project, New York.

- Chris Natrop, *Fern Space Burst*, 2004, hand cut paper, colored ink, watercolor, iridescent medium, tape, and thread, 10 x 8x 8 feet. Courtesy of the Artist.

- Robyn O'Neil, *This is a descending world*, 2007, graphite on paper, 14 x 22 inches. Courtesy of the Artist and Clementine Gallery, New York.

- Laura Owens, *Untitled* (LO 233d), 2003, acrylic, pencil, and collage on paper, 24 x 18 inches. Collection of Matt Aberle. Courtesy of the Artist and Gavin Brown's enterprise, New York; *Untitled* (LO 306d), 2005, watercolor, pencil, pastel on paper, 14 x 10 1/4 inches. Collection of Martina Yamin. Courtesy of the Artist and Gavin Brown's Enterprise, New York.

- Raymond Pettibon, *Untitled (It was fine…)*, 1991, ink on paper, 24 ½ x 18 inches. Courtesy of the Artist and Rita Krauss Fine Art, New York.

- Chloe Piene, *Careful Hand*, 2007, charcoal on vellum, 12 x 9 inches. Courtesy of the Artist and SandroniRey, Los Angeles.

- Amy Rathbone, *Rainbags*, 2005, ink and gouache on paper, 22 x 30 inches. Courtesy of the Artist and Gregory Lind Gallery, San Francisco. On loan from Priska Juschka Fine Art, Los Angeles.

- Clare Rojas, *Untitled (woman holding flower)*, 2007, gouache and latex on panel, 12 x 12 inches. Courtesy of the Artist and Gallery Paule Anglim.

- Gina Ruggeri, *Overgrowth*, 2005, acrylic on mylar, 42 x 87 inches; *Hole*, 2005, acrylic on mylar, 42 x 82 inches. Courtesy of the Artist and Kevin Bruk Gallery, Miami.

- Paul Rutkovsky, *Smile*, 2001, pen and ink, 7 x 8 inches; *Can You Learn*, 2001, pen and ink, 7 x 8 inches; *Muscle Head*, 2005, pen and ink, colored pencil, 7 x 8 inches; *Merry to the End*, 2005, pen and ink, colored pencil, 7 x 8 inches. Courtesy of the Artist.

- Andrew Schoultz, *Trampled Under Hoof*, 2007, mixed media on paper, 7 x 9 feet; *Untitled* site-specific installation for Florida State University Museum of Fine Arts. Courtesy Morgan Lehman Gallery, New York, and Heather Marx Gallery, San Francisco.

- Tucker Schwarz, *Nothing can save me now*, 2005, thread on muslin, 30 x 49 inches; *Somehow it never seems to be quite enough*, 2005 thread on muslin, 24 x 36 inches; *Well I suppose that explains everything*, 2005, thread on muslin, 38 ½ x 48 ½ inches. Courtesy of the Artist and Gregory Lind Gallery, San Francisco.

- Kirsten Rae Simonsen, *Running Scared*, 2007, charcoal, pencil, acrylic, and gesso on wood panel, 11 x 14 inches. Courtesy of the Artist.

- Kiki Smith, *Woman on Pyre*, 2001, ink on Nepal paper, 61 x 75.5 inches; *Pyre*, 2001, ink on Nepal paper, 77.5 x 70 inches. Courtesy of the Artist and PaceWildenstein, New York.

- Swoon, *Helena*, 2006, relief print and spray stencil on mylar, 32 ½ x 71 ½ inches. Courtesy of the Artist and Deitch Projects, New York.

- Yuken Teruya, *Notice Forest (Graz Zweitausenddrei)*, 2006, paper bag, 4 ½ x 9 ¾ x 16 inches. Courtesy of the Artist and Shoshana Wayne Gallery, Santa Monica.

- Pae White, *Noisy Letters (Blue)*, *Noisy Letters (Green)*, *Noisy Letters (Yellow)*, 2006, collage, 37 x 25 inches. Courtesy of the Artist and 1301PE, Los Angeles.

- Wendy Wischer, *Longing*, 2004, cut paper, 18 x 16 inches diameter; *Sunspot diaries*, 2003, paper burned with magnifying glass and sunlight, 30 x 40 inches. Courtesy of the Artist and David Castillo Gallery, Miami.

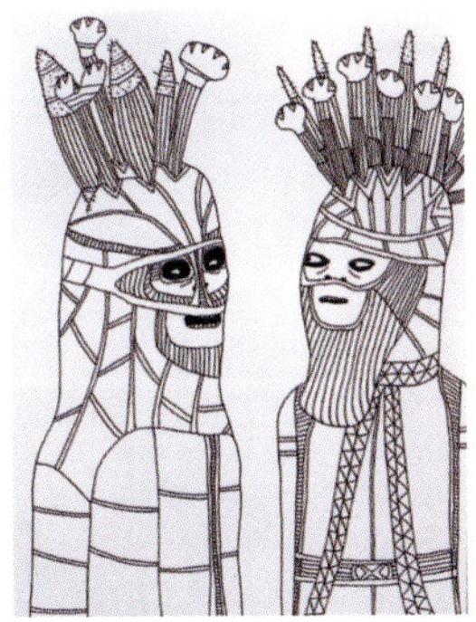

## LAYLAH ALI

*At once endearing, twisted and sophisticated, Laylah Ali's work has long played on the ways we type people—whether by skin color, costume or behavior. Her compelling gouache paintings feature figures in a generally cheerless and nicely designed universe whose background tends to milky sky blue. By giving her characters a variety of skin colors—brown, black, green, sometimes all three—she lets us know, cryptically but with more than a little humor, that race is an issue in her work. And by equipping her bug-eyed characters with neat-looking apparel—pointy Klan hats, Adidas sneakers, medieval headgear, nun habits, striped tube socks, bathing trunks, even Band-aids—she not only enlivens her compositions, but also tweaks our impulse to use such visual cues to figure out who these people are and what is going on.*

—excerpted from Sarah Valdez, "Laylah Ali at 303," *Art in America* 93 (May 2005): 166.

Laylah Ali lives and works in Williamstown, Massachusetts. She is represented by 303 Gallery, New York.

Selected Exhibitions: 2007—*Laylah Ali: Drawing from the Typology Series,* Pennsylvania Academy of Fine Arts, Philadelphia (touring to: University of Iowa Museum of Art, Iowa City; University of Arizona Museum of Art, Tucson). Solo Exhibition, Institute of International Visual Arts, London. *Alien Nations,* Institute of Contemporary Art, London; Manchester City Art Gallery; Sainsbury's Art Center, Norwich. 2005—*Typology,* Gertrude Contemporary Art Space, Melbourne, Australia. 2004—Solo Exhibition, Contemporary Art Museum, St. Louis, MO. *Whitney Biennale 2004,* The Whitney Museum of American Art, New York, NY. *Material Witness,* The Museum of Contemporary Art, Cleveland, OH. *Walker Without Walls,* outdoor billboard project, with Walker Art Museum, Minneapolis, MN. 2003—Solo Exhibition, Albright-Knox Gallery, Buffalo, NY. *Crosscurrents at the Century's End: Selections from Neuberger Berman Art Collection,* Henry Art Gallery, Seattle, WA (touring to: Norton Museum of Art, West Palm Beach, FL; Tampa Museum of Art, Tampa, FL; Chicago Cultural Center, Chicago, IL). 2002—Solo Exhibition, Museum of Modern Art, New York, Project 75. 2000—Solo Exhibition, MassMOCA, North Adams, MA. 1998—*Selections Summer '98,* Drawing Center, New York, NY.

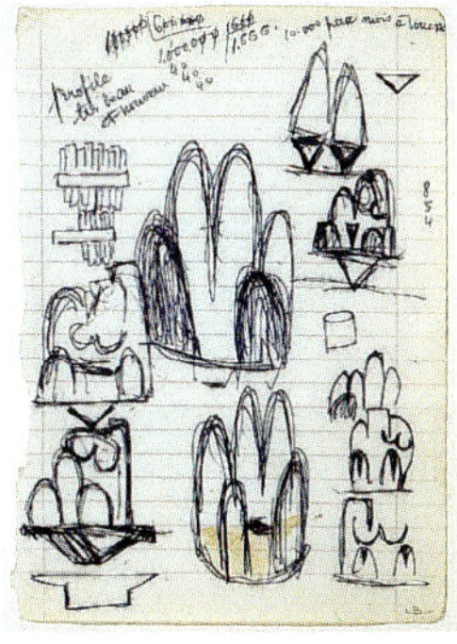

## LOUISE BOURGEOIS

*Unlike some artists who use drawing to develop plans for larger projects, Bourgeois has always treated her graphic works as independent compositions. With their characteristic hatched lines, spare detail, and neutral backgrounds, the drawings nevertheless address themes also seen in her sculpture, including isolation, love, loss, and beauty. Bourgeois has described them as "ideas and little complaints." Made using pen, pencil, crayon, and gouache, the drawings range in style from colorful figures to muted abstractions. Even at their most inventive, Bourgeois' drawings are meant to represent the dramas of everyday living.*

—excerpted from press release for *Drawings by Louise Bourgeois* at the Saint Louis Art Museum, 2004.

Louise Bourgeois lives and works in New York City.

Selected Exhibitions: 2000—Solo Exhibition, National Museum of Contemporary Art, Korea. *The American Century: Art & Culture,* 1950-2000, Whitney Museum of American Art, New York. 1999—Solo Exhibition, Museuo Nacional Centro de Arte-Reina Sofia, Madrid. *Regarding Beauty: A View of the Late 20th Century,* Hirshhorn Museum and Sculpture Garden, Washington. *Whitney Biennial,* Whitney Museum of American Art, New York. Wexner Center Honoree. Golden Lion, Board of La Biennale di Venezia, 48th International Exhibition of Art. Praemium Imperiale Award of Japan. 1996—Commission for Battery Park City Authority for the Robert F. Wagner, Jr. Park, New York. National Medal of Arts presented by President Clinton. 1993—Mayor's Award for Art & Culture, New York. *Venice Biennale,* represented United States. 1991—Lifetime Achievement Award, International Sculpture Center, Washington D.C. (first recipient). Grand Prix National de Sculpture awarded by the French Ministry of Culture.

Laylah Ali, *Untitled,* 2004, ink on paper, 9 ½ x 7 ½ inches (LA 134). Courtesy 303 Gallery, New York.

Louise Bourgeois, *Untitled,* 1971, ink on lined paper, 8 x 5 ¾ inches. Courtesy of the Artist and Cheim & Read, New York.

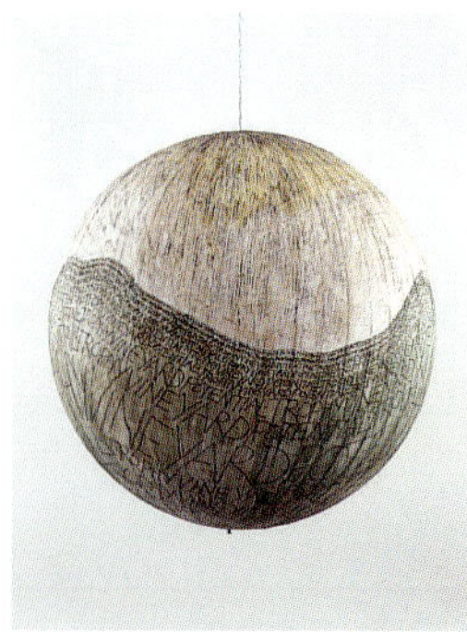

## RUSSELL CROTTY

*Russell Crotty studies the California nocturnal skies from his observatory, which is housed in a roll-off-roof shed fit with a 10" reflecting telescope. This observatory, set atop one of the tallest peaks on the Pacific Coast Highway, offers a 360° view of ocean, mountain and sky.*

*Crotty has been producing books for many years, beginning with a series of surf books. These books, which painstakingly chronicled a protagonist surfer's daily rides, were investigations in obsessive-compulsive doodling…The drawings, although focused on planets, moons, and stars, often include depictions of desert and alpine flora as well. More recently, however, Crotty muses on the encroaching suburbia which threatens to light up the sky; the astronomer's worst nightmare.*
—excerpted from Shoshana Wayne Gallery press release, 2000.

Russell Crotty lives in Upper Lake, California, where he built the Solstice Peak Observatory. He is represented by Shoshana Wayne Gallery, Los Angeles and by CRG Gallery, New York.

Selected Exhibitions: 2006—*Twilight in the West*, Hosfelt Gallery, San Francisco. *Fallout: Cold War Culture*, Mitchell-Innes & Nash, New York. 2005—Solo Exhibition, Suzanne Tarasieve Gallery, Paris. Solo Exhibition, Centre d'Art Contemporain, Rennes, France. *Messages & Communications*, The Mattress Factory, Pittsburgh. 2004—*A Grain of Dust, A Drop of Water*, Gwangju Biennale, South Korea. *National Drawing Invitational*, Arkansas Art Center, Little Rock. 2003—*Globe Drawings*, Kemper Museum of Contemporary Art, Kansas City, MO (touring to: Miami Art Museum, Miami). 2002—Solo Exhibition, CRG Gallery, New York. *Drawing Now: Eight Propositions*, Museum of Modern Art, Queens. *LA Post-Cool*, San Jose Museum of Art, San Jose. *Personal Plans: The Drawing—from Life Plan to World Projection*, Kunsthalle Basel, Switzerland. *Drawing on Space*, The Drawing Room, London. 2001—*The Universe: The Universe From My Backyard*, Williamson Gallery, Art Center College of Design, Pasadena, CA.

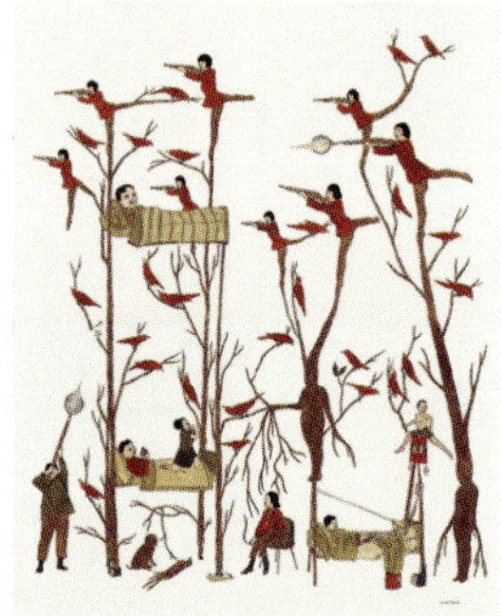

## MARCEL DZAMA

*When you first see the art of Marcel Dzama, you may feel you are looking at illustrations from some quaintly antique children's book. He specializes in pen-and-ink drawings in which pale, slender women routinely meet up with rabbits and talking trees. Yet Dzama isn't making art for children.*

*He uses his innocent-looking style to capture a savage contemporary universe, a place that is grimmer than any Grimm's tale. It's as if you have wandered off the proverbial path to grandmother's house and stumbled upon some secret internment camp where bossy personality types (men with rifles, flying bats) oversee the wounded and the weak.*

*Dzama is a Canadian Wunderkind, and his lugubrious fairy-tale sensibility in some way exemplifies the latest drift in contemporary art. Call it cute tragedy or tragic cuteness: either way, it refers to the impulses of a post-Warhol generation that uses the popular art forms of childhood to express a startling array of adult feelings.*
—Deborah Solomon, "Drawn to Trouble," *New York Times Magazine*, 4 September 2005.

Marcel Dzama lives and works in New York. He is represented by David Zwirner, New York.

Selected Exhibitions: 2007—Solo Exhibition, *Celluloid Ceremony*, Galerie Magnus Karlsson, Stockholm, Sweden. Solo Exhibition, *Moving Picture*, Timothy Taylor, London, UK. 2006—Solo Exhibition, *Marcel Dzama*, Sies + Höke, Düsseldorf, Germany. Solo Exhibition, *Marcel Dzama: Tree with Roots*, IKON, Birmingham, UK (touring to: Centre for Contemporary Arts, Glasgow, Scotland). Solo Exhibition, *Marcel Dzama*, The Richard L. Nelson Gallery & The Fine Arts Collection, UC / Davis, Davis, CA. 2005—Solo Exhibition, *The Course of Human History Personified*, David Zwirner, New York. Solo Exhibition, *The Lotus Eaters*, Centre d'Art Santa Monica, Barcelona, Spain. *New Work / New Acquisitions*, The Museum of Modern Art, New York. 2004—Solo Exhibition, *Marcel Dzama*, Sies + Höke, Düsseldorf, Germany. *Marcel Dzama*, Olga Korper, Toronto, Canada. *Funny Cuts: Cartoons and Comics in Contemporary Art*, Staatsgalerie Stuttgart, Stuttgart, Germany. 2003—*Royal Art Lodge: Ask the Dust*, The Drawing Center, New York (touring to: Power Plants, Toronto; De Vleeshal and De Kavinetten can De Vleeshal, Middleburg, the Netherlands; Seoul Museum of Art, Seoul, South Korea; Elaine L. Jacob Gallery, Wayne State University, Detroit; The Museum of Contemporary Art, Los Angeles). *The Great Drawing Show 1550- 2003*, Michael Kohn Gallery, Los Angeles. *Zwischenbilanz*, Kunstforum Baloise, Basel, Switzerland. 2002—*Fantasy Underfoot*, Corcoran Biennial, Washington, DC. *La Biennale de Montreal 2002*, Montreal, Quebec. 2000—New Artists Award, Art Cologne.

---

Russell Crotty, *Vineyard Potential*, ink and watercolor on paper mounted on fiberglass, 12 inch diameter. Courtesy of the Artist and CRG Gallery, New York.

Marcel Dzama, *Eight Strong Winds*, 2005, ink and watercolor on paper, 4-part drawing, each drawing 14 x 11 inches, 28 x 22 inches overall. Private Collection, New York. Courtesy of David Zwirner, New York.

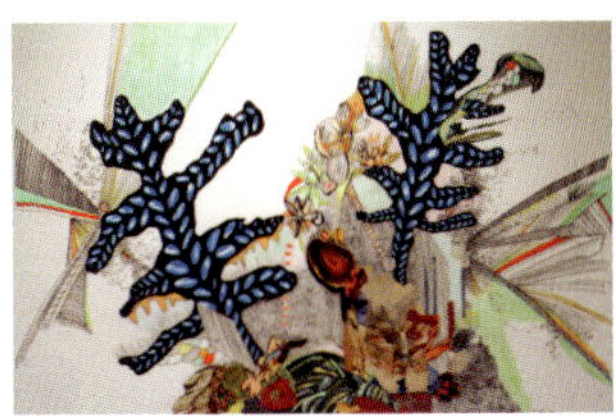

## JANAE EASTON

*Developing and supporting the contradictions in desire, beauty, friction, neediness, betrayal, loss, and love. I am interested in both chaos and order, discord and pleasure.*

*This tension between the images becomes a point of interest. The distance between the marks, the overlapping touch of materials, the almost touch, the I cannot let go touch. The process reiterates the compulsion of need; I create a forest of obsessive marks that consume, overload, over stimulate, splatter, repeat to become a new environment.*

*My work creates a community of marks. Nature triggers the work; in the drawings I am trying to create details that evoke the slow and rapid growth in nature. My process connects with the ambiguity of the organic world but is also inspired by surrealism, landscape painting, assemblage, storytelling, how to books, flower arranging, graffiti, cake decorating, flea markets, art brut, and the idea of slowness.* —JE

Janae Easton lives and works in Tallahassee, Florida.

Selected Exhibitions: 2007—*Flower Power Invitational*, Gadsden Arts Center, Quincy, FL. New 07, NURTUREart Gallery, Brooklyn. 2006—*Drawings from Another Time: Past to Present*, Lakefront at Landon Gallery, University of Wisconsin. *New Work, New Faces*, Museum of Fine Arts, Florida State University, Tallahassee. Puffin Foundation Ltd. Grant. 2005—*Night of 1,000 Drawings*, Artist Space, New York. *Postcards from the edge*, New York. *House of Cards*, Carriage House, Columbus, OH 2004—*The Land of Growth*, book making workshop and exhibition, Nan Boynton Gallery, Tallahassee. *Cycles: Janae Easton and Kristin Miller*, College of Southern Maryland, LaPlata, MD. *Small Victories*, Modest Contemporary Arts Project, Chicago. 2003—*Morphological Construction*, Nan Boynton Gallery, Tallahassee. *Douglas Dribble Memorial Art Auction*, Hunter College Time Square Gallery, New York.

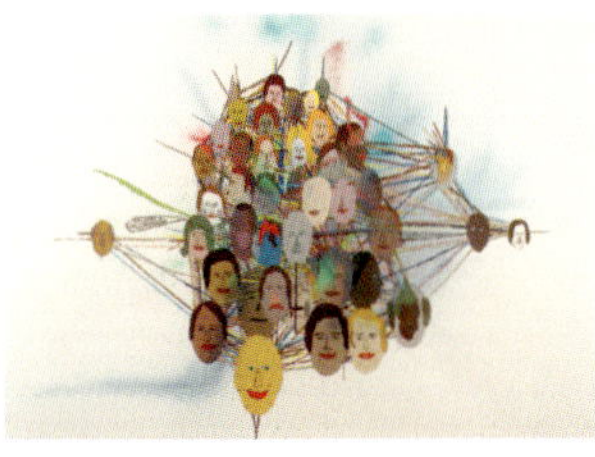

## CHRIS JOHANSON

*Fully immersed in this brave and groovy new world (especially to a kid from suburban San Jose), Johanson began obsessively making quick painterly sketches on found wood and recycled canvases. His early works were predominantly in black and white, and often laced* with simple but prophetic text that reflected the gritty drama he witnessed on the streets of the downtrodden, yet culturally fertile, Mission District. The sketches depicted people wandering aimlessly, grasping to fill tattered souls with drugs and alcohol and power and material things; praying, flailing in piss puddles, looking for a moment of salvation, or even just a fleeting sense of okayness despite all evidence to the contrary.

At a glance, Johanson's visual style appears a half-notch above stick figure, coyly naive, but his sense of composition is flawless and extremely sophisticated, and what's more, his message takes aim at all sides of the human condition with an unrelenting gravitas. Johanson's art is an art of ideas that far exceeds the sum of his brush strokes. Over the years, his aesthetic has never stopped evolving. Johanson almost compulsively adds to his repertoire: a full spectrum of color, coarsely rendered sculptural installations, video, tinfoil, huge helium balloons, and, more recently, a surge into abstraction and modernism, all without ever losing the inimitable Johanson-ness at the core of the work.

—excerpted from Arty Nelson, "He Walks the Line: Chris Johanson finds the space between humor, hatred, and love" *LA Weekly Magazine*, June 7, 2006.

Chris Johanson lives and works in Portland, Oregon. He is currently represented by Jack Hanley Gallery in San Francisco and Kavi Gupta Gallery in Chicago.

Selected Exhibitions & Awards: 2007—Solo Exhibition, Portland Art Museum, Portland. *Art Unlimited*, Art Basel, Basel, Switzerland. 2006—Solo Exhibition, Kavi Gupta Gallery, Chicago. Solo Exhibition, Jack Hanley Gallery, Los Angeles. *Of Mice and Men*, 4th Annual Berlin Biennial for Contemporary Art, Berlin. 2005—*Beautiful Losers*, Orange County Museum of Art, Orange County, CA. 9th International Istanbul Biennale, Istanbul. 2004—*Solo Exhibition*, The Modern Institute, Glasgow, Scotland. Solo Exhibition, Museum of Contemporary Art San Diego, San Diego. 2003—Solo Exhibition, San Francisco Museum of Modern Art, San Francisco. Statements Booth, *Art Basel*, Basel Switzerland. *Baja to Vancouver: The West Coast and Contemporary Art*, Seattle Art Museum, Seattle (touring to: Museum of Contemporary Art San Diego; Vancouver Art Gallery, Vancouver, BC; and CCA Wattis Institute for the Arts, San Francisco). 2002—Solo Exhibition, Deitch Projects, New York. *Whitney Biennial*, Whitney Museum of American Art, New York. 2001—Solo Exhibition, UCLA Hammer Museum, Los Angeles.

---

Janae Easton, Detail of *Fragrant Meadows*, 2006, mylar, paper, found papers, pen, colored marker, colored pencil, graphite, 23 x 33 inches. Courtesy of the Artist.

Chris Johanson, *Untitled (I am what is called human)*, 2005, acrylic on paper, 34 x 47 ¾ inches. Courtesy of the Artist and Kavi Gupta Gallery, Chicago.

## LOS CARPINTEROS

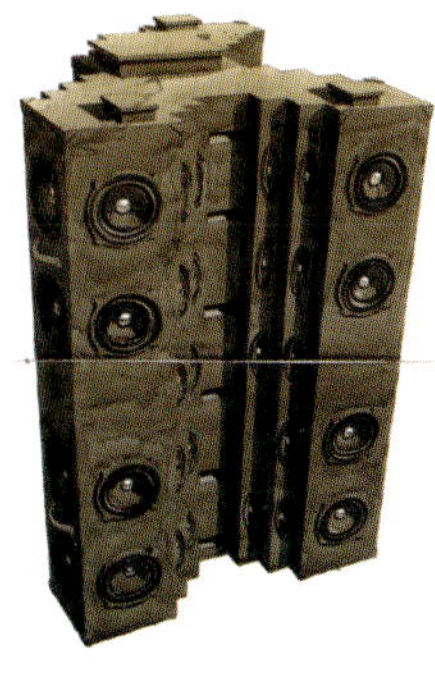

*Los Carpinteros' works on paper deal almost entirely with buildings and their materials—resonant subjects in Cuba, with its decaying infrastructure. The group also conflates architectural structures with furniture, in a hilarious if sometimes unsettling mixture of the domestic and the public. Working in a style of skilled realism, with plump lines and sweeping strokes of gouache that skirt as close to illustration as drafting, Los Carpinteros produce both finished drawings for their own sake and to-scale working drawings for at least theoretically buildable (though half-size)* public buildings and monuments. Although these works relate to sculpture and sculptural ideas, the artists specify that the drawings are not precisely preparatory; as Rodriguez puts it, they are "neither cause nor effect."

—excerpted from Laura Hoptman, *Drawing Now: Eight Propositions* (Museum of Modern Art, 2002).

Marco Antonio Castillo Valdés and Dagoberto Rodríguez Sánchez live and work in Havana, Cuba. The artists are represented internationally by Galeria Habana, Havana; Galeria Fores Vilaca, Sao Paulo, Brazil; and Sean Kelly Gallery, New York.

Selected Solo Exhibitions: 2007—*Piscina Casa (Home Pool)*, Le Grand Café–Centre d'Art Contemporain de Saint-Nazaire. 2006—*Sel et Poivre*, Galerie In SITU, Paris, France. Faro Tumbado, Galería Habana, Havana. *Los Carpinteros*, Contemporaneamente, Milan, Italy. *Los Carpinteros*, Unosunove and IILA, Rome. 2005—*Los Carpinteros: Inventing the World*, University of South Florida Contemporary Art Museum, Tampa (touring to: Chicago Cultural Center, Chicago; Contemporary Arts Center, Cincinnati; Museum London, London). *En el Jardin*, Fortes Vilaça Gallery, São Paulo. 2004—*Downtown,* Anthony Grant Inc., New York. *Manual de Trabajo, dibujos. Esculturas Recientes*, Galería Servando Cabrera, Havana. 2003—*Novos Desenhos*, Fortes Vilaça Gallery, São Paulo. *Fluido*, Museo Nacional de Bellas Artes, Havana. 2002—*Los Carpinteros intervention at B. Opening,* Baltic The Center for Contemporary Art, New Castle, England. *Ciudad Transportable*, Contemporary Art Museum of Hawaii, Honolulu. 2001—*Túneles Poplares,* Palacio de Avrahante, Salamanca, Spain. *Los Carpinteros*, Caleria Camargo Valaça, São Paulo. *Cuidad Transportable,* P.S.1 Contemporary Art Center, Long Island. *Los Carpinteros*, Grant Selwyn Fine Art, Los Angeles. *Cuidad Transportable*, Los Angeles County Museum of Art, Los Angeles. *Los Carpinteros*, San Francisco Art Institute, San Francisco. 2000—*Los Carpinteros*, Grant Selwyn Fine Arts, Los Angeles. 1999—*Tania Bruguera/Los Carpinteros*, Vera Van Laer Galerie, Antwerp, Belgium. 1998—*Los Capinteros. Project Room, Fiera Internacional de Arte Contemporáneo ARCO '98*, Parque Ferial Juan Carlos I, Madrid. *Mecánica Popular*, Galería Habana, Havana. *Los Carpinteros*, Ludwig Forum für Internationale Kunst, Achen, Kusthalle, Berlin. *Bili Bidjocka/Los Carpinteros/Rivane Neunschwande*, The New Museum of Contemporary Art, New York. *Los Carpinteros*, Iturralde Gallery, Los Angeles.

## BARRY MCGEE

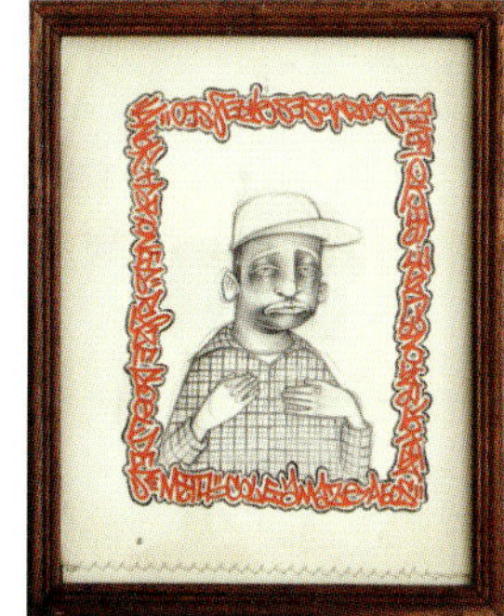

*McGee creates works directly on "found" surfaces ranging from the gallery walls to steel printer's trays, from discarded bottles to scraps of paper mounted in thrift-store frames. Entangled in a sea of floating hardware, calligraphic markings, and fragmented body parts, his wall installations infuse a sublime poetic order on the inner city. These large-scale, site-specific works reference the ambivalent citizenry of the city through astute juxtapositions of figurative imagery reminiscent of Mad magazine and Dr. Seuss illustrations,* which address "urban ills, over stimulations, frustrations, addictions, and trying to maintain a level head under the constant bombardment of advertising."

*A prolific producer of public works, McGee employs the materials, aesthetic vocabulary, and performativity of graffiti for his works. Inspired by his own civic participant/observer role, his invocation of graffiti writing recasts our understanding of discrete objects, action painting, temporality, and the use of text in Conceptual Art. The resulting mural-scale installations suggest a distressed, though markedly absurd contemporary horizon.*

—excerpted from press release for *Regards, Barry McGee* at the Walker Art Center, Minneapolis, July 1998.

Barry McGee resides in San Francisco, California. He exhibits at Gallery Paule Anglim, San Francisco, and Paul Morris Gallery, New York.

Selected Exhibitions: 2007—Solo Exhibition, Watari Museum of Contemporary Art, Tokyo, Japan. *American Art in China,* Guggenheim Museum, New York and MoCA, Shanghai. 2006—*We Have Some Friends in Common*, Nicolai Wallner Gallery, Copenhagen. *Spank the Monkey*, BALTIC Centre for Contemporary Art, Gateshead. 2005—*One More Thing*, Deitch Projects, New York, NY. *Things Are Really Getting Better*, March Museum Het Domein Dittard, Netherlands. 2004—Solo Exhibition, Rose Art Museum, Brandeis University, Boston, MA. Solo Exhibition, Prada Foundation, Milan. *Beautiful Losers*, The Contemporary Arts Center, Cincinnati, OH. 2002—*Liverpool Biennale*, Liverpool. *Drawing Now*, Museum of Modern Art, New York, NY. 1998—*Regards, Barry McGee*, Walker Art Museum, Minneapolis, MN. 1996—SECA Award Installation, San Francisco Museum of Modern Art, San Francisco, CA.

---

Los Carpinteros, *Alto Parlante—Cohiba* (diptych), 2007, watercolor on paper, 60 1/4 x 44 inches (LC-07D009). Courtesy of Sean Kelly Gallery, New York.

Barry McGee, *Untitled*, 1998, pencil and marker on paper, 9 7/8 x 8 inches. Courtesy of the Artist and Paul Morris Gallery, New York.

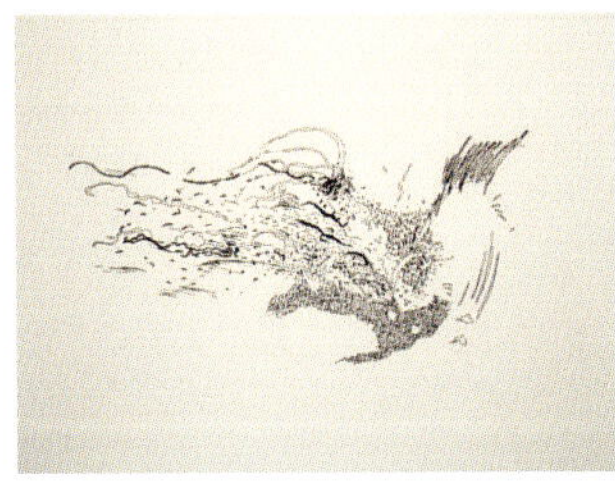

### JULIE MEHRETU

*Mehretu has developed an idiosyncratic system of dots, dashes, arrows, circles, crosses, squares, curlicues and organic shapes which she repeats in dense, built-up passages suggesting fragments of a large, albeit ambiguous, narrative. Her signs are expressively charged, much as van Gogh's abstract marks carry personal emotion even as they coalesce into representation. Mehretu's frenetic forms swirl, float and march as they burst through numerous spatial envelopes—overlaying, underlying and intersecting crisp, delicately drawn lines. Bands, parallelograms and arcs of color torque the picture space and bring the multiplanar activity up to the surface. Her works are epic dramas, as lyrical as they are combustible, that deconstruct conventional notions of space and time.*
　　　　　　　—excerpted from Susan Harris, "Julie Mehretu at The Project,
　　　　　　　"*Art in America* 90 (March 2002): 122.

Julie Mehretu lives and works in New York City where she is represented by The Project.

Selected Exhibitions: 2007—*Julie Mehretu: Black City*, Kunstverein Hannover, Hannover, Germany. American Academy in Berlin Fellowship. 2006—*Julie Mehretu: Heavy Weather*, Crown Point Press, San Francisco, CA and The Print Center, Philadelphia, PA. The Rhode Island School of Design Alumni Council Artistic Achievement Award, Rhode Island. *Zones of Contact: The 15th Biennale of Sydney*, Sydney, Australia. *The Compulsive Line: Etching 1900 to Now*, Museum of Modern Art, New York, NY. 2005—MacArthur Fellow. American Art Award, Whitney Museum of Art, New York, NY. *Currents 95: Julie Mehretu*, St. Louis Art Museum, St. Louis, MO. 2004—*Carnegie International*, Carnegie Museum of Art, Pittsburgh, PA. *Sao Paulo Bienal*, Sao Paulo, Brazil. *Whitney Biennial*, Whitney Museum of American Art, New York, NY. 2003—*Julie Mehretu: Drawing into Painting*, Walker Art Center, Minneapolis, MN (touring to: REDCAT, Los Angeles, CA and Albright-Knox Art Gallery, Buffalo, NY.) *Poetic Justice- 8th International Istanbul Biennial*, Istanbul.

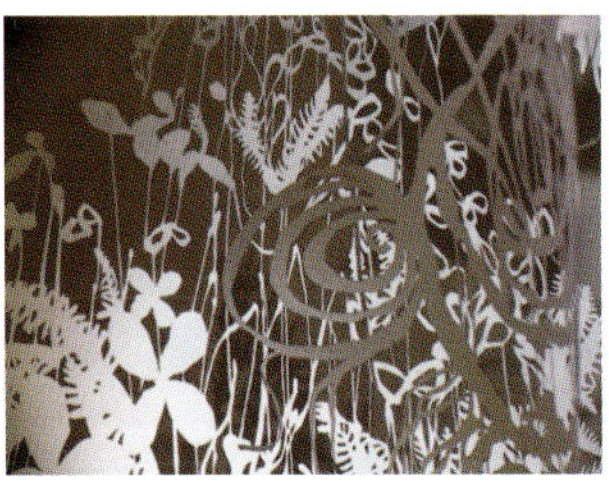

### CHRIS NATROP

*The work of Chris Natrop becomes a beautiful "quasi-utopia" (as he calls it) which rewards the viewer with infinite opportunities to get lost in a private cosmos. In these labor-intensive works, Natrop's cuts are not pre-determined; he relinquishes control and allows the work to grow itself as he navigates his way across the page. The process of "getting lost" is a Buddhist ideal. While this work is clearly secular in nature, walking into the installation to be among these elegant forms is an opportunity to reflect on something larger than the self.*
　　　　　　　—Rebecca Niederlander, *Artscene Los Angeles* (December 2006)

Chris Natrop lives and works in Los Angeles. He is represented by Bank, Los Angeles.

Selected Exhibitions: 2007—*Pulse Art Fair*, New York (awarded "Pulse Prize"). *Lost in Space*, Chapman Univerity, Orange, CA. 2006—*Into the Silver See-Through*, Bank, Los Angeles. *fern space blast*, Sonoma County Museum, Santa Rosa, CA. *white white mayday in mustard and gold*, Raid Projects, Los Angeles. *Aqua Art Fair*, Bank, Miami Basel event, Miami Beach. 2005—*11 1/2, Overtones*, Los Angeles. *scope art fair*, Yoo Projects, New York. 2004—Affiliate Artist, Headlands Center for the Arts, Sausalito, CA. *spring paper twist*, LiveArt Gallery, San Francisco. *Happy Art for a Sad World*, Spike Gallery, New York. 2003—*Fault Lines*, Windhover Center for the Arts, Fond du Lac, WI. *Linkage, An installation by Chris Natrop*, Melting Point Gallery, San Francisco. *New American Artists*, Galleria Ruggieri, Genoa, Italy. *X-Zincografia*-Open Space, Venice, Italy.

---

Julie Mehretu, *Untitled*, 2001, ink on mylar and paper, 19 x 20 inches. Collection of Christian Haye. Courtesy of The Project, New York.

Chris Natrop, Detail of *Fern Space Burst*, 2004, hand cut paper, colored ink, watercolor, iridescent medium, tape, thread, 10 x 8 x 8 feet. Courtesy of the Artist.

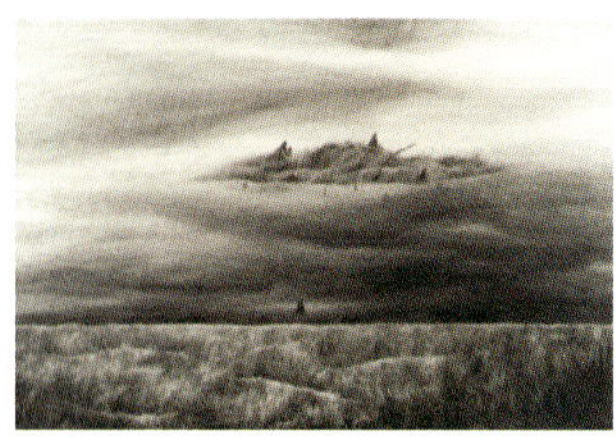

### ROBYN O'NEIL

*Robyn O'Neil's graphite on paper drawings, alternately epic and intimate, always intricate and precise, have cumulatively imagined a realm characterized by pervasive anxiety and melancholy beauty, where the threat (or promise?) of death may be the most powerful constant across her oeuvre. This is a descending world. makes explicit from its titular selection forward that this ongoing struggle between, at its simplest, good and evil is pushing for final resolution. The apocalypse has arrived, and it may offer some strange relief to the relentless, anxious current of fear and judgment that streams through all of O'Neil's work.*

—excerpted from "This is a descending world" catalog essay by Shamim Momin.

Robyn O'Neil lives and works in Houston, Texas and exhibits at Clementine Gallery, New York.

Selected Exhibitions: 2006—*Perspectives 150: Robyn O'Neil,* Contemporary Arts Museum, Houston, TX (touring to: Frye Art Museum, Seattle, WA; Herbert F. Johnson Museum of Art, Cornell University, Ithaca, NY). *Robyn O'Neil,* Galerie Praz- Delavallade, Paris. 2005—*And Then They Were Upon Him,* Bodybuilder & Sportsman Gallery, Chicago, IL. *Trials and Terrors,* Museum of Contemporary Art, Chicago, IL. 2004—*Whitney Biennial,* Whitney Museum of American Art, New York, NY. 2003—*Artadia Grant,* Artadia- The Fund for Art and Dialogue, New York, NY. International Artist in Residence, ArtPace Foundation for Contemporary Art, San Antonio, TX. *Artissima 10 art fair,* Inman Gallery, Turin, Italy. *The Company We Keep,* Inman Gallery, Houston, TX. 2002—*Bad Touch,* Ukrainian Institute of Modern Art, Chicago, IL. *Drawn II,* Barry Whistler Gallery, Dallas, TX. *Postcards from the Edge,* Visual AIDS Benefit, Sperone Westwater Gallery, New York, NY. *These are Pictures of Boats and Dinosaurs,* Angstrom Gallery, Dallas, TX. 2000—*small abstract paintings and sculpture,* Eugene Binder, New York, NY. *Positexan…the show with the right attitude,* Project, Wichita, KS.

### LAURA OWENS

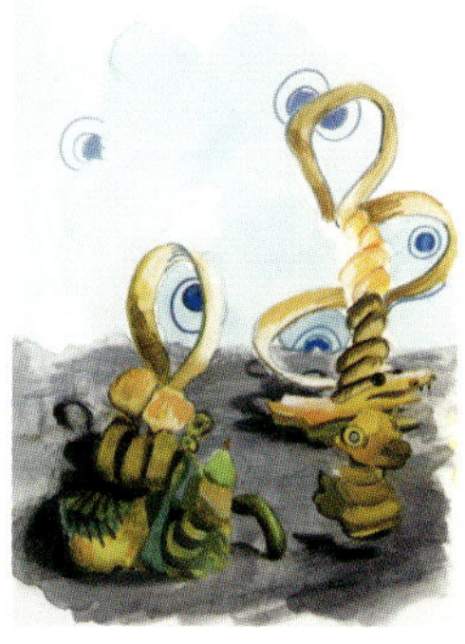

*In an era when many younger artists struggle with issues of heroism and the weight of achievements past, Los Angeles-based painter Laura Owens seems to have opened her umbrella and floated over the art historical baggage collecting on the tarmac. Owens borrows where she pleases—from modernist movements past such as Color Field, Op Art, and Pattern and Decoration, from European painters like Rousseau and Toulouse-Lautrec, from anonymous mediums such as textile and embroidery. Art historical references and any sort of imagery, high or low, that Owens feels like incorporating are co-opted with finesse and a clear-eyed sense of no-fuss entitlement, in service to a larger goal: her own precise vision for what makes a painting pleasurable to behold. Despite this precision she is highly versatile, and her paintings vary from abstraction to figuration to kooky nature landscapes in which the animals cohabitate in a harmony that limns the absurd.*

—Introduction to an interview with the artist by Rachel Kushner.

Laura Owens lives and works in Los Angeles, CA. She is represented by Gavin Brown's enterprise, New York; Sadie Coles HQ, London; Galerie Gisela Capitain, Cologne; and ACME, Los Angeles.

Selected Exhibitions & Awards: 2007—*Sequence I, Paintings and Sculpture from the Pinault Collection,* Palazzo Grassi, Venice, Italy. Solo Exhibition, Bonnefanten Museum, Maastricht (touring to: Ausstellungshalle zeitgenössische Kunst, Münster; Camden Arts Centre, London; Kunsthalle Zürich, Zürich). 2006—*Essential Painting,* Osaka National Museum of Art, Osaka. 2005—Solo Exhibition, Shiseido Gallery, Japan. 2004—Solo Exhibition, Fabric Workshop and Museum, Philadelphia. *Whitney Biennial 2004,* Whitney Museum of American Art, New York. 2003—Solo Exhibition, Milwaukee Art Museum, Milwaukee (touring to: Aspen Art Museum, Aspen; Museum of Contemporary Art, Los Angeles; Museum of Contemporary Art, North Miami). 2002—*Cavepainting: Peter Doig, Chris Ofili, and Laura Owens,* Santa Monica Museum of Art, Santa Monica. *Drawing Now: Eight Propositions,* The Museum of Modern Art, New York. 2001—*Painting at the Edge of the World,* Walker Art Center, Minneapolis. 2000—*New Work by Laura Owens (1999) and John Hutton Balfour's Botanical Teaching Diagrams (1840–1879),* Inverleith House, Royal Botanic Garden, Edinburgh. *American Academy Invitational Exhibition of Painting and Sculpture,* The American Academy of Arts and Letters, New York.

---

Robyn O'Neil, *This is a descending world,* 2007, graphite on paper, 14 x 22 inches. Courtesy of the Artist and Clementine Gallery, New York.

Laura Owens, *Untitled,* 2005, watercolor, pencil, pastel on paper 14 x 10 1/4 inches. Collection of Martina Yamin. Courtesy of the Artist and Gavin Brown's enterprise, New York.

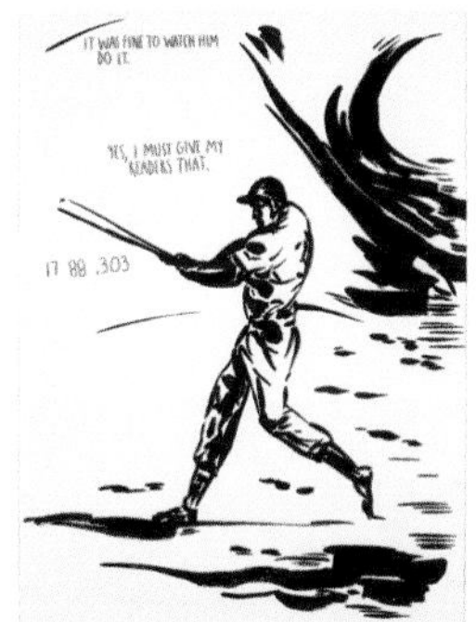

### RAYMOND PETTIBON

*Growing up, looking at the comic page in the morning is a mindless chore, as natural as brushing our teeth. Then one day we become aware of the benday dot's role, its materiality, its existence. We could kick ourselves for not knowing better, for not seeing it until then. The Pop artists enacted this moment for the culture as a whole. They stood up to the hollow heroism of Abstract Expressionism and the dogmatic critical discourse of the day and unmasked the illusions of representation. Sneaking their appropriated figures in the back door of formalism, they peeled back a veneer to show us that all was a sham. What the Pop artists did by co-opting the language of commercialism for their own "different, appealing" art was honest and new. When I started copying from TV, movies, or magazines, however, I had no illusions I was doing anything original. I wasn't even trying to be ironic or kitsch. Comics and illustrations simply worked well as a universal means of expression. I didn't feel I had to revisit or belabor the idea of mechanical reproduction. (So even if, from across the room, you might mistake one of my drawings for a Lichtenstein study, as you draw closer, you see a giveaway. I gave those damn dots up years ago for traditional rendering: illusionistic cross-hatches judiciously applied, with brush or pen, so you hardly notice 'em). Today it's no longer necessary to frame that material, footnote it, or make apologies for it. We already know representations, however feebly drawn, are still representations, and therefore illusions that delude both subject and audience.—RP*

Raymond Pettibon lives and works in Hermosa Beach, California. He is represented by David Zwirner, New York, and Rita Krauss Fine Art.

Selected Exhibitions: 2007—*Raymond Pettibon*, Sadie Coles HQ, London. *Half Square/Half Crazy*, Villa Arson, Nice. 2006—*Into Me/Out of Me*, KW Institute for Contemporary Art, Berlin, Germany (traveling to: MARCO, Rome). *Red Eye. L.A. Artists from the Rubell Family Collection*, Rubell Family Collection, Miami, FL. *Raymond Pettibon*, Contemporary Art Center Malaga, Malaga, Spain. *Raymond Pettibon, Whatever it is you're looking for you won't find it here*, Kunsthalle Wien, Vienna, Austria. 2005—Solo Exhibition, Whitney Museum of American Art, New York, NY. *Raymond Pettibon*, Contemporary Fine Arts, Berlin, Germany. *Thrust- The 26th Biennal of Graphic Arts*, Ljubljana, Slovenia. 2004—*100 Artists See God*, Naples Museum of Art, Naples, FL (touring to: The Jewish Museum San Francisco, San Francisco, CA; Laguna Museum, Laguna Beach, CA; Memorial Art Gallery, University of Rochester, Rochester, NY). Bucksbaum Award, Whitney Museum of American Art, New York. *Raymond Pettibon*, Galleria d'Arte Moderna, Bologna, Italy. 2003—*Raymond Pettibon. Plots laid thick*, Gemeentemuseum, The Hague, Netherlands. *Raymond Pettibon. Drawings 1979-2003*, MUSEION, Bozen, Italy.

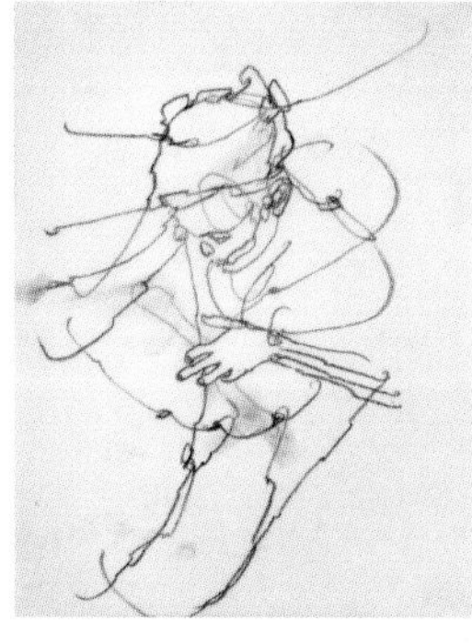

### CHLOE PIENE

*Chloe Piene's drawings inhabit and extend the German expressionist mood that oftentimes invents sharply delineated, visionary features in order to portray a human body that skirts along the boundaries between the physical and metaphysical worlds. Her charcoal on vellum drawings frequently depict cropped or only partly rendered bodies. These delicately drawn bodies appear as skeletal forms, scarcely covered with flesh and tissue. As a result, Piene's subjects appear to be caught in transitional states of corporeality, where and when the exact separation between the solid and the atmospheric becomes indistinct.*

*Piene approaches drawing with a purity and singularity that bucks the traditional framework in which drawing has lain. Her two major media, video and drawing, simultaneously display aspects of delicacy and brutality.*
                    —excerpted from SandroniRey press release, 2005.

Chloe Piene lives and works in Berlin and New York. She is represented by SandroniRey, Los Angeles.

Selected Exhibitions: 2007—Solo Exhibition, *Chloe Piene*, Le Musée des Beaux-Arts, Nimes, France. Solo Exhibition, *Chloe Piene*, Witte de With, Rotterdam, Netherlands. Solo Exhibition, Alon Segev Gallery, Tel Aviv, Israel. Two Person Exhibition, *Chloe Piene and William de Kooning*, Locks Gallery, Philadelphia, PA. 2006—*ARS06*, Kiasma, Helsinki, Finland. *Street: Behind the Cliche*, Witte de Withe, Rotterdam, The Netherlands. 2005 – Solo Exhibition *Part I (Drawing) and Part II (Video)*, Sandroni Rey, Los Angeles, CA. Solo Exhibition, *Chloe Piene*, Galerie Nathalie Obadia, Paris, France. *Getting Emotional*, Institute of Contemporary Art, Boston, MA. *Will Boys Be Boys?*, Museum of Contemporary Art, Denver, CO, CAMH, Houston, TX, and Salinas Art Center, Salinas, KS. 2004—Solo Exhibition, *Chloe Piene*, Kunsthalle Bern, Bern, Switzerland. *Boys Behaving Badly*, Contemporary Arts Museum, Houston, TX. *Whitney Biennial*, Whitney Museum of American Art, New York, NY.

---

Raymond Pettibon, *Untitled (It was fine…)*, 1991, ink on paper, 24 ½ x 18 inches. Courtesy of the Artist and Meridian Gallery, New York. Photo credit: Jon Nalon.

Chloe Piene, *Careful Hand*, 2007, charcoal on vellum, 12 x 9 inches. Courtesy of the Artist and SandroniRey, Los Angeles.

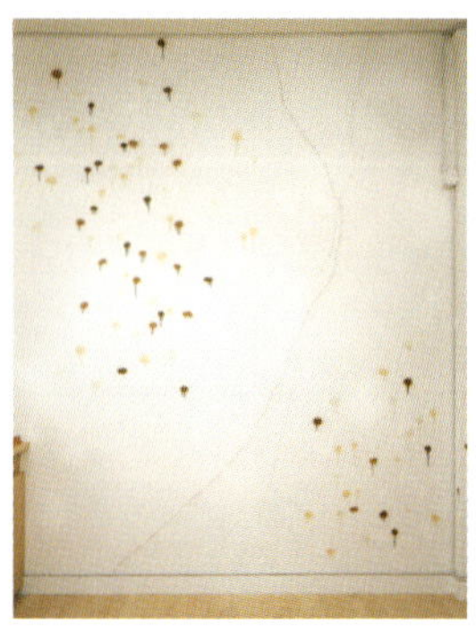

### AMY RATHBONE

*San Francisco-based Amy Rathbone has become known for subtle site-specific installations that interact with various galleries' architecture, as well as for her enigmatic drawings. At times she has created installations that transform an entire room into a simple single artwork....*

*One of the best wall works was Let's Face It. With coffee-colored stains that dripped down the wall, patches of short black wires sticking out like beard stubble, and random drips of darker colors, it evoked a bleary-eyed hung-over feeling. Less noticeable were spots and drips of a white that was slightly lighter than the wall color, creating the effect of bathtub soap scum streaked by bleach. . . .*

*Rathbone's works are not particularly demanding or self-important, but their delicate nature and insouciance quietly merit attention.*
—Stephanie Cash, "Amy Rathbone at Priska C. Juschka,"
*Art in America* 94 (May 2006): 186-187

Amy Rathbone lives and works in San Francisco where she is represented by Gregory Lind Gallery.

Selected Exhibitions: 2006—*unbent*, Priska C. Juschka Fine Art, New York, NY. *ZusammenKunst*, Galerie Hafemann, Wiesbaden, Germany. 2005—*probably raw*, Memorial Union Art Gallery, University of California at Davis. *Realms of San Francisco*, Nakaochiai Gallery, Tokyo, Japan. *Water Color: Current Views*, Gallery Joe, Philadelphia, PA. *Fix Box*, RARE Gallery, New York, NY. 2004—*on one side of the river, healthy desires; on the other a measly phone booth*, Gregory Lind Gallery, San Francisco, CA. *All Four Corners*, Maryland Art Space, Baltimore, MD. *Pink Steam*, Eureka Space, San Francisco, CA. 2003—*Windows*, Jack Hanley, San Francisco, CA. *Makeshift World*, Steven Wirtz Gallery, San Francisco, CA. *The Peace Show*, Adobe Brooks, San Francisco, CA. 2002—*Under the Circumstances*, a.o.v. San Francisco. *EMERGE*, Gen Art, San Francisco, CA. *Introductions*, Braunstein/Quay Gallery, San Francisco, CA.

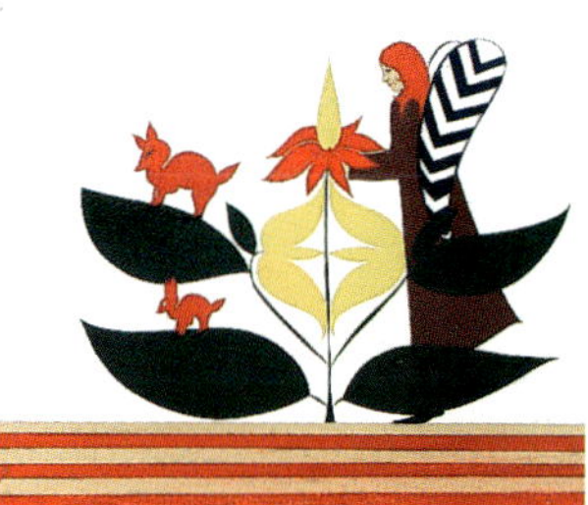

### CLARE ROJAS

*Throughout her work [Rojas] develops a personal, esoteric folklore with repeating characters that interact and travel through landscapes and environments. These whimsical, dreamlike panel paintings and drawings at first appear innocent, yet possess a fairy tale-like darkness lurking just beneath the surface. In Rojas's world, unexpected meetings between little girls and androgynous characters, monsters, and personified animals occur in surreal lands dotted with misplaced trees and flowers. The songs that Peggy Honeywell writes and performs are inextricably linked to the paintings: the rambling lyrics are sweet and melodic, yet melancholic, a corollary text and soundtrack that complement Rojas' unique visual vocabulary.*
—excerpted from "'Clare Rojas' on View through July 31,"
San Francisco Art Institute press release, 2004.

Clare Rojas lives and works in San Francisco, California. She exhibits with Gallery Paule Anglim, San Francisco, and Kavi Gupta Gallery, Chicago.

Selected Exhibitions: 2007—*Clare Rojas, Hope Springs Eternal*, Rose Art Museum, Brandeis University, Waltham, MA. 2006—Solo Exhibition, Ulrich Museum of Art, Wichita State University, Wichita, Kansas. *Clare Rojas*, Nicolai Wallner Galeri, Copenhagen, Denmark. 2005—*Hah! Ha, ha, ha!*, Kavi Gupta Gallery, Chicago. *Clare Rojas*, Modern Art, London. *Sub-Urban: Clare Rojas*, Knoxville Museum of Art, TN. Eureka Fellowship Award Exhibition, Berkley Art Museum, California. *Beautiful Losers*, Orange County Museum of Art, Orange County (touring to: Yerba Buena Center for the Arts, San Francisco; Contemporary Arts Center, Cincinnati, OH). 2004—*Table Turner*, Deitch Projects, New York. Tournesol Award, one year residency, Headlands Center for the Arts, Sausalito, CA. 2002—*Doing My Day*, Museum of Contemporary Art, Chicago. *Maybelle Crick*, Lizabeth Oliveria, San Francisco. *Walk Like Man*, New Image Art, Los Angeles.

---

Amy Rathbone, *Plebians*, 2004, spray enamel, wire and pencil on wall, dimensions variable. Courtesy of the Artist and Gregory Lind Gallery, San Francisco.

Clare Rojas, *Untitled (woman holding flower)*, 2007, gouache and latex on panel, 12 x 12 inches. Courtesy of the Artist and Gallery Paule Anglim.

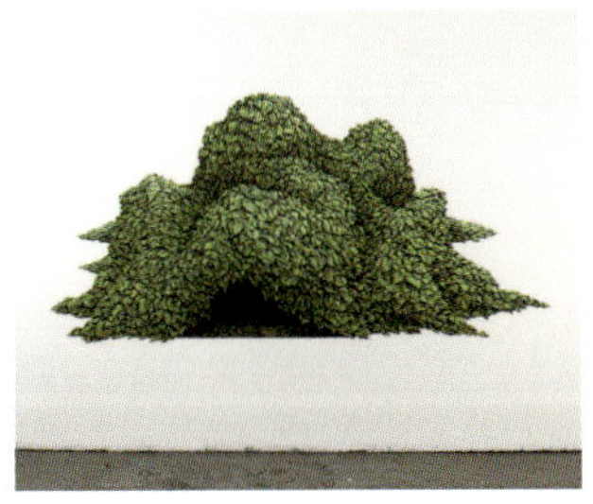

### GINA RUGGERI

*These Mylar cut-out paintings incorporate the wall itself into their pictorial illusion. Attached seamlessly to the wall's surface, the images appear to float in an atmospheric field of white. The flat silhouettes of highly dimensional forms are scaled to life-size and installed low on the wall, creating a spatial continuum between the viewer and the image.*

*Although they appear "real", the forms are entirely fictional, invented through a process of drawing visualization. Constructed from my imagination, the everyday subjects have an concrete yet emblematic quality, like a memory or dream image. Natural and man-made objects seem inhabited or alive, and often imply a trace of human interference, suggesting a narrative that lies beyond what is represented.—GR*

Gina Ruggeri is an Adjunct Assistant Professor at Vassar College, Poughkeepsie, New York. She is represented by Kevin Bruk Gallery, Miami, Florida, and Lyons Wier Ortt Contemporary, New York.

Selected Exhibitions: 2007—*The Eclectic Eye: Selections from the Frederick R. Weisman Art Foundation,* Contemporary Art Center, New Orleans, LA. Fellowship, VCCA Artist Residency, Amherst, VA. 2006—*Gina Ruggeri: New Paintings,* Kevin Bruk Gallery, Miami, FL. *Queens International 2006,* Queens Museum of Art, Flushing, NY. Fellowship, Yaddo Artist Residency, Saratoga Springs, NY. Fellowship, Jentel Artist Residency, Banner, WY. 2005—Special Editions Fellowship, The Lower East Side Printshop. 2004—*Gina Ruggeri: New Work,* Kevin Bruk Gallery, Miami, FL. 2003—*Gina Ruggeri: New Paintings,* Red Dot, New York, NY. *Guest Artist Exhibition,* Tenri Biennale, Tenri, Japan. 2002—*Gina Ruggeri: New Work,* Vassar College, Poughkeepsie, NY. Grant Recipient, The Marie Walsh Sharpe Art Foundation Space Program.

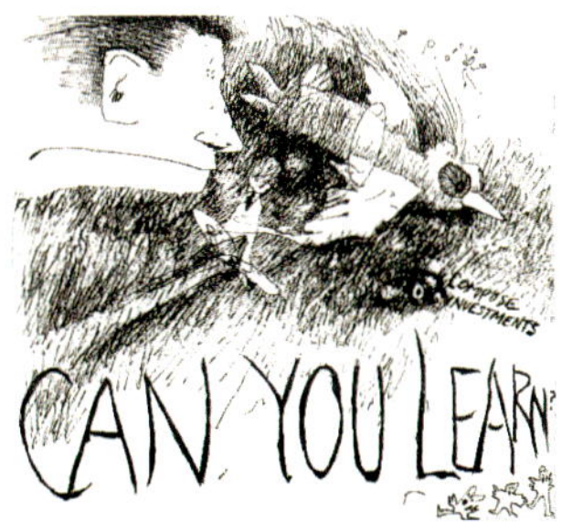


### PAUL RUTKOVSKY

*My work incorporates low and high tech consumer appliances, motors with rotating plastic hamburgers, consumer products covered with thousands of branches, display racks full of garbage, drawings, or computer prints with thick dripping paint, fans cooling motors that overheat, cassette players with continuous sounds of television commercials and soap operas, toys that frown, toys that smile, and toys that talk, all revealing my connection to a manufactured world of plastic, blood, and tissue. Whether I'm working with young students in Poland using computers, HIV-positive individuals in Syracuse, collecting debris with students in Lithuania, Latvia and Finland, or art students at Florida State University, the primary focus for me is to connect the technology to our lives, to eliminate the barriers between flesh and silicon. —PR*

Paul Rutkovsky lives and works in Tallahassee, Florida.

Selected Exhibitions: 2008—Solo Exhibition, Akademija Gallery, Vilnius Academy of Fine Arts, Vilnius, Lithuania. 2007—*Draw Small Think Big,* Profile Gallery at The Centre of Culture, Poznan, Poland. 2006—*Transient,* ON Gallery, Poznan, Poland. 2005—*Reduce/Reuse/Reexamine,* Wave Hill Glyndor Gallery, Bronx, NY. 2004—*Refuse: Functional Art Objects & Music Made from Waste,* Flux Factory, Long Island City, NY. 2002—*Speaking Volumes,* Book Arts Invitational, American Museum of Papermaking, Atlanta, GA. *Earth 2002,* New Gallery, University of Miami, Miami, FL. 1991—Artist-In-Residence, Light Work, Syracuse, NY. 1989—Harvard University, Fellow, Summer Institute for the Avant-Gardes, Cambridge, MA. 1988—MacDowell Colony Fellow, Peterborough, NH. 1987—Massachusetts Institute of Technology, Fellow, Cambridge, MA. 1980—National Endowment for the Arts Fellowship.

---

Gina Ruggeri, *Overgrowth*, 2005, acrylic on mylar, 42 x 87 inches. Courtesy of the Artist and Kevin Bruk Gallery, Miami.

Paul Rutkovsky, *Can you Learn*, 2001, pen and ink, 7 x 8 inches. Courtesy of the Artist.

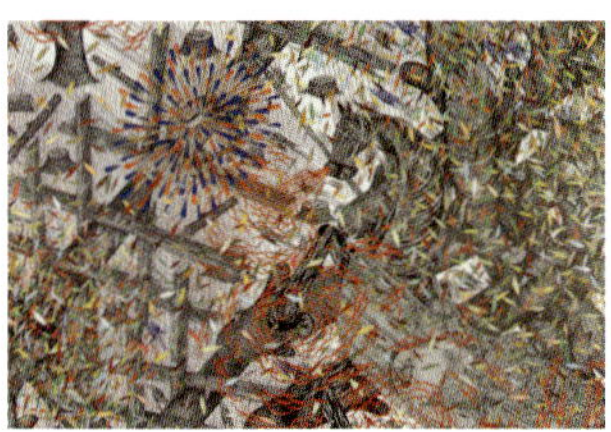

## ANDREW SCHOULTZ

*Art is an uncontrollable passion and obsession. After many travels around the United States for such things as skateboarding and graffiti art, I found a home in San Francisco in 1997, and among other things, a great community to exist in and make art. The past nine years have brought me the development of a repertoire of iconic images. Through murals, paintings, installations, and drawings, I have used these images to tell stories about everyday life in America, filtering political commentary through the forms of graffiti art and underground comics, fused with clip-art from the early 1900s and medieval rendering that chart the history of man and nature. The relationship between man and nature has been a re-occurring theme in my work, and also the effects of globalism and capitalism on the world. Although heavily interested in showing work and doing large multi-media installations in the gallery and museum setting, I have spent a tremendous amount of time doing murals and various work in the street of America and abroad. I have an intense interest in painting large scale imagery on walls in the public space, that address and inform the very diverse audience of the general public, including children, about social and political issues.—AS*

Andrew Schoultz is a San Francisco based artist who exhibits at Morgan Lehman Gallery, New York, and Heather Marx Gallery, San Francisco.

Selected Exhibitions: 2007—*Common Denominator*, Whitewalls Gallery, San Francisco, CA. 2006—*Loud and Quiet*, Taylor Decordoba Gallery, Los Angeles, CA. *Flow Art Fair*, Morgan Lehman Gallery, Miami, FL. *Casualties of Convenience*, Giant Robot, New York, NY. *Cartoon Networks*, RAID Projects, Los Angeles, CA. 2005—*Oracles and Ruminations*, Sara Nightengale Gallery, Watermill, NY. *Mayhem*, 15th Annual Juried Exhibition, Southern Exposure, San Francisco, CA. *New Work*, Scope New York Art Fair, Yoo Projects, New York. 2004—*Linescapes*, Bucheon Gallery, San Francisco, CA. *Work…ethic*, Space Gallery, Portland, ME. *Carpe Cras*, two person show with Ryan Wallace, Black Market Gallery, Culver City, CA. Kennedy Park Mural Project, Portland, ME. April/May. 2003—*The Artwork of Andrew Schoultz*, And Gallery, St. Paul, MN. *Wall Paintings*, two person show with Aaron Noble, Track 16 Gallery, Santa Monica, CA. 2002—*Bloom Town*, Bucheon Gallery, San Francisco, CA. Solo Exhibition, Anno Domini, San Jose, CA.

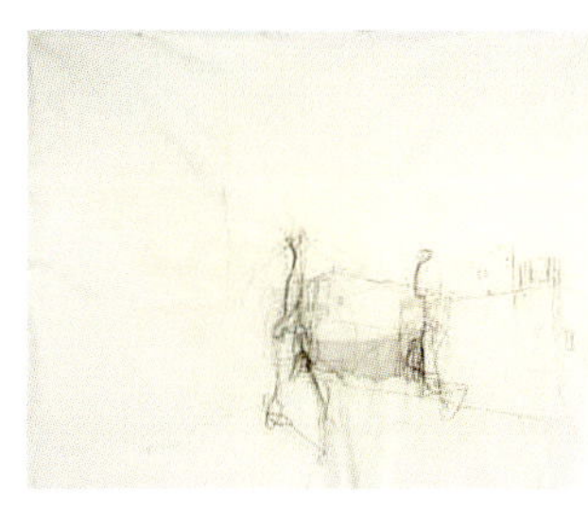

## TUCKER SCHWARZ

*I use a sewing machine to "draw" on fabric. The images are based on photographs I have taken and bits of personal memory. The photographs are taken while walking or driving through a neighborhood or a land-scape. All the images are seen from a distance and are literally coming apart. Many of the threads are left dangling and often lines are not completed. I am interested in subtle, quiet images that trigger our memories and emotions.*

*In addition to the sewn drawings, I have begun to explore three- dimensional installations. I am utilizing the same materials, but instead the "drawings" are abstract and composed in space rather than sewn directly onto the canvas. They maintain a fragile and even more delicate structure that suggests things are only loosely held together. The unraveling nature of the drawings is mimicked in the knots and fraying ends of the threads used in the installations. I am very interested in the interconnectedness and links made in these networks of thread and the implicit metaphor of falling apart if even one should be untied.—TS*

Tucker Schwarz lives and works in San Francisco where she is represented by Gregory Lind Gallery.

Selected Exhibitions: 2007—*The HandMaking*, Abington Art Center, Jenkintown, PA. *Graphic: New Bay Area Drawing*, diRosa Preserve: Art & Nature, Napa, CA. 2005—*I'm sure I'm shouting*, Gregory Lind Gallery, San Francisco, CA. *New Found Land*, Priska Juschka Fine Art, New York, NY. *New Tapestries*, Sara Meltzer Gallery, New York, NY. *Close Calls*, Headlands Center for the Arts, Sausalito, CA. 2004—Djerassi Resident Artist Program, Woodside, CA. 2003—*Place Particular*, Black Bird Space, San Francisco, CA. *Sewn Together*, Gregory Lind Gallery, San Francisco, CA. 2002—*I know I shouldn't, but I do*, Nexus Gallery, Philadelphia, PA. *She's Crafty (and so is he sometimes)*, White Columns, New York, NY. 2001—*Tucker Schwarz and Neil Rasmussen*, 1Pixel, Philadelphia, PA. *No regrets*, Southern Exposure, San Francisco, CA. *The Cat's Away*, Sara Meltzer Gallery, New York, NY.

---

Andrew Schoultz, Detail from *Communication Destruction*, 2007, ink, acrylic, and collage on paper, 38 x 52 inches. Courtesy of Morgan Lehman Gallery, New York, and Heather Marx Gallery, San Francisco.

Tucker Schwarz, *Well I suppose that explains everything*, 2005, thread on muslin, 38 ½ x 48 ½ inches. Courtesy of the Artist and Gregory Lind Gallery, San Francisco.

## KIRSTEN RAE SIMONSEN

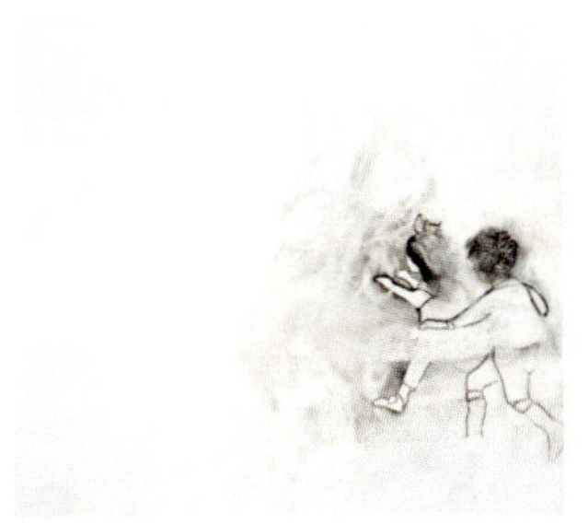

*My work is concerned with transgression and debasement. I find inspiration in the more menacing rhymes and stories from traditional children's books such as Mother Goose, as well as Victorian era English school books. I study and represent in my work the way gender roles and expectations are formed at an early age in these books.*

*I am also interested in the idea of children as trangressors, as entities that act out of turn, whose behavior does not always fall into the realm of acceptable social behavior. Animals also appear in my work, and exhibit similar "bad behavior." Trying to fit either children or animals into a polite and predictable society inevitably leads to some sort of social disorder.*—KS

Kirsten Rae Simonsen spends winters in Honolulu and summers in Amsterdam. She is represented by Whitespace Gallery in Atlanta and Domo Gallery in Summit, New Jersey.

Selected Exhibitions: 2007—*21st Annual International Juried Show*, Visual Arts Center of New Jersey, Summit, NJ. *National Drawing 2007*, The Gallery of the College of New Jersey, Ewing, NJ. Flatfile: Artspace, New Haven, CT. 2006— *Now or Neverland*, The Residence Gallery, London. *Future First History Last*, The Residence Gallery, Hackney, London. 2005—*Be Home Before Dark*, The Residence Gallery, Hackney, London. *The 19th Drawing Show*, Mills Gallery at the Boston Center for the Arts, Boston. *3rd Annual Seattle Erotic Art Festival*, Seattle. 2004—Atlantic Center for the Arts, Artist Residency, New Smyrna Beach, FL. Solo Exhibition, *Peaceable Kingdom*, Peter Miller Gallery, Chicago. *Master's Mystery Show*, Art Basel Miami 2004 Event, Miami. 2003—*My Generation, Part II*, Peter Miller Gallery, Chicago. *This is Not Me*, ARC Gallery, Chicago.

## KIKI SMITH

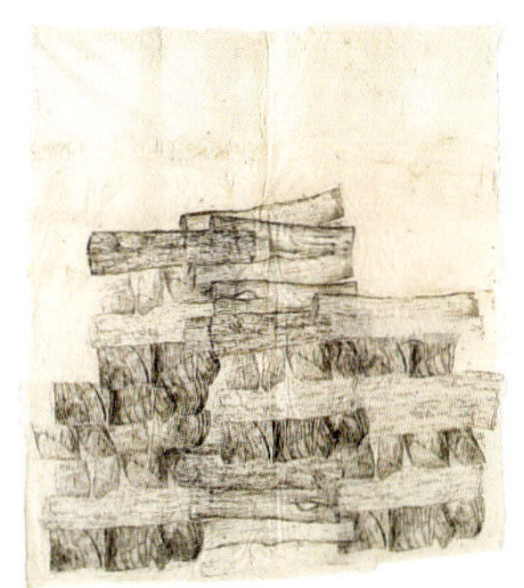

*Kiki Smith has an uncanny knack for transforming the mundane into the enchanted. She uses whatever materials suit her purpose, from blood to bronze and from glitter to glass. Her art takes the form of drawing, printmaking, sculpture, photography, books, performance, sound, video, jewelry, and costume design, among others.*

*Most of Smith's visual art is related to the body and to the natural world. It often has a handmade quality to it, and it is deeply rooted in a tradition of art that values the final object as a marriage between vision and craft. Despite a strong physicality, her work also has a palpable spiritual component. She continually weaves together the internal and external, the physical and spiritual, the personal and collective.*

—excerpted from The Whitney Museum of American Art website, text by Carrie Springer.

Kiki Smith lives and works in New York City where she has exhibited with PaceWildenstein since 1994.

Selected Exhibitions: 2006—*A Gathering, 1980-2005*, San Francisco Museum of Modern Art (traveled to: Walker Art Center, Minneapolis; Contemporary Arts Museum, Houston, TX; Whitney Museum of American Art, New York, NY; La Colección Jumex, Mexico City). Solo Exhibition, Contemporary Arts Museum, Houston, TX. Solo Exhibition, Whitney Museum of American Art, New York, NY. *Contemporary Voices: Works from the UBS Art Collection*, The Museum of Modern Art, New York, NY, traveled to: The Fondation Beyeler, Basel, Switzerland. 2005—Elected to the American Academy of Arts and Letters, New York, NY. *Homespun Tales, Storie di occupazione domestica*, Fondazione Querini Stampalia, Venice. 2004—*Art of the 1990s from the Logan Collection*, San Francisco Museum of Modern Art, San Francisco, CA. *Prints, Books & Things*, The Museum of Modern Art, Queens, NY. 2003—*Homework*, The Fabric Workshop and Museum, Philadelphia, PA. 2002—*Whitney Biennial 2002*, Whitney Museum of American Art, New York, NY. 2000—Skowhegan Medal for Sculpture.

Kirsten Rae Simonsen, *Running Scared*, 2007, charcoal, pencil, acrylic, and gesso on wood panel, 11 x 14 inches. Courtesy of the Artist.

Kiki Smith, *Pyre*, 2001, ink on Nepal paper, 77.5 x 70 inches. Courtesy of the Artist and PaceWildenstein, New York.

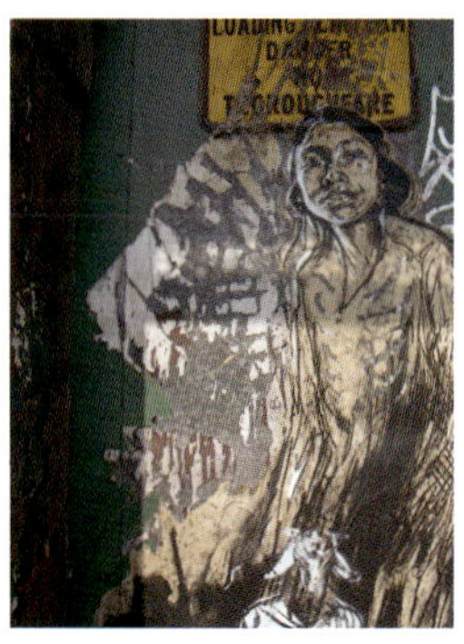

## SWOON

*Swoon began working with the streets of New York City about six years ago, with projects ranging from billboard alterations, and poster campaigns, to street parties and sculptural installations. Her focus has been on creating a lively public realm that relies not on bureaucratic channels of permission, but on the direct action of citizens who wish to be a constant force in the creation of the environment they live in. Her most intensive project has been a series of life sized posters utilizing block printing and cut paper to create portraits of city life which are then pasted back into the environments that inspired them. She started the collective Toyshop about three years ago and has been traveling for the past two years creating exhibitions and workshops in the United States and Europe. Other collaborators include Brooklyn based art collectives, Glowlab, Black Label, Change Agent, the Madagascar Institute and the Barnstormers.*

Swoon lives and works in New York City where she is represented by Deitch Projects.

Selected Exhibitions & Awards: 2007—*The Burning House*, New Image Art Gallery, Los Angeles. 2006—*Generations UsA*, Pinchuk Art Center, Kiev. *La Boaca del Lobo*, Black Floor Gallery, Philadelphia. 2005—Two person exhibition with Os Gemeos, Deitch Projects, Miami. *Project Backjumps Part 2*, Kunstraum Kreuzberg, Berlin. *Swoon*, Deitch Projects, New York. 2004—*Something Else*, The Vinyl Factory, London. *Ill Communication II*, Urbis, Manchester, UK. *1:100*, DCKT Contemporary, Manhattan. *Ever Wanting Streets*, Roda Sten, Gothenburg, Sweden. *Change Agent, Call it a Crew*, Space 1026, Philadelphia. *Good World*, Publico, Cincinnati. 2003—*Project Backjumps*, Kunstraum Kreuzberg, Berlin. 2002—*Swoon loves Solovei*, Urban-Art.info, Berlin. Evolutionaere-Zellen grant recipient, NGBK, Berlin.

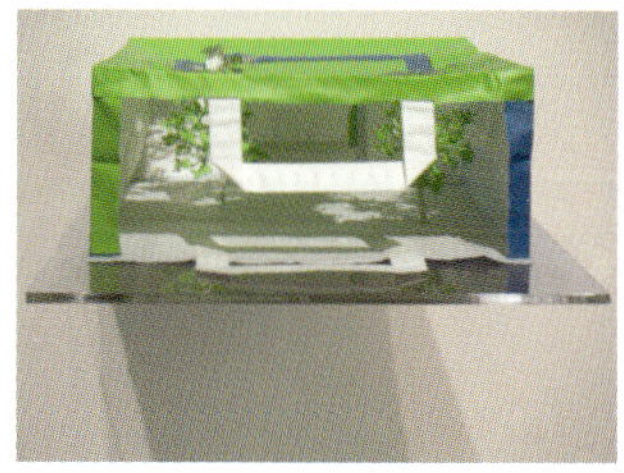

## YUKEN TERUYA

*Yuken Teruya manipulates everyday objects, transforming their meanings to reflect on contemporary society and culture. Central features of his works include the idea of metamorphosis, and the subversion of expectations or traditional meanings.*

*Using a variety of materials and media—from kimonos, to pizza boxes, newspaper articles, shopping bags and paper-cuttings—Teruya frequently creates meticulous and intricate art works, small and enchanting worlds, which relate to broader concerns. Teruya's works explore issues such as the growing consumerism of contemporary society, depleting natural resources and other problems associated with globalism, including the threat it poses to localised cultural traditions and identities.*

—excerpted from the press release for the 5th Asia-Pacific Triennial of Contemporary Art 2007.

Yuken Teruya lives and works in New York. He is represented by Shoshana Wayne Gallery, Santa Monica, CA, and Josee Bienvenue Gallery, New York.

Selected Exhibitions: 2007—*The Shapes of Space*, Solomon R. Guggenheim Museum, New York. 2006—*Asia-Pacific Triennial*, Queensland Art Gallery, Queensland, Australia. *Bangladesh Biennial*, Dhaka. 2005 —NYFA Fellowship for Sculpture. *VOLTAshow*, Basel, Switzerland. Solo Exhibition, Kunstverein Weisbaden, Germany. *Altoid's Curiously Strong Collection*, The New Museum of Contemporary Art, New York, NY. *Yokohama International Triennial*, Yokohama, Japan. 2004—*Refrain*; Korean, Balkan, Okinawa Total Museum of Contemporary Arts; Seoul, Korea. Solo Exhibition, Diverseworks, Houston, TX. *Fuchu Biennale*, Fuchu Art Museum, Tokyo, Japan. 2003—*Okinawan Contemporary Art*, Naha City Gallery, Okinawa, Japan. 2002—Vision of Contemporary Artists, Tokyo, Japan. Solo Exhibition, The Aldrich Museum of Contemporary Art, Ridgefield, CT.

---

Swoon, *Helena*, 2006, relief print and stencil on paper, 32½ x 71½ inches. Courtesy of the Artist and Deitch Projects, New York.

Yuken Teruya, *Notice Forest (Graz Zweitausenddrei)*, 2006, paper bag, 4 ½ x 9 ¾ x 16 inches. Courtesy of the Artist and Shoshana Wayne Gallery, Santa Monica.

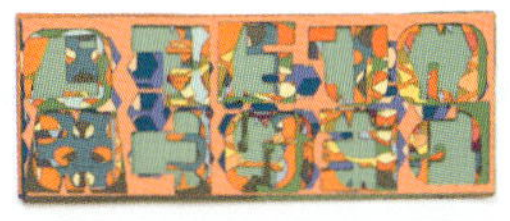
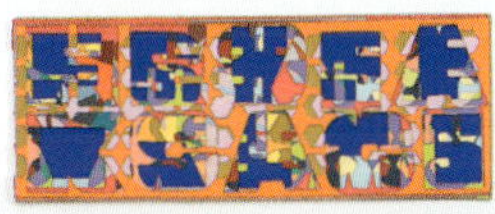
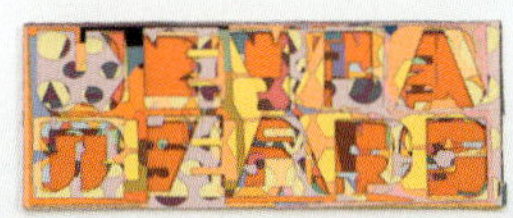

### PAE WHITE

*Pae White belongs to a generation of international artists who have revived issues of site and context that have remained largely unexplored since the mid-1970s. Although at times you find her work where you would expect it—that is, at eye level on walls or somewhere central on the floor—you are just as likely to find it covering windows, suspended in midair, or stacked up around a corner between two rooms. Often you won't find it in exhibition spaces at all, but in areas of museums and galleries dedicated to* activities other than the display of art: the bookshop window (Galerie Daniel Buchholz, Cologne), for instance, the office (China Art Objects, Los Angeles), a children's learning area (Los Angeles County Museum of Art), or foyer (the Hammer piece you've just been looking at). It undergoes a more extreme process of dispersal when it takes the multiple format of covers for magazines (four issues of Make: Women's Art Magazine), advertisements for galleries (a series of twelve for neugerriemschneider in Frieze), or invitation cards and catalogs for other artists' exhibitions (Jorge Pardo and Tobias Rehberger, for example).*

—excerpted from Hammer Projects press release, 2004,<br>text by Alex Farquharson.

Pae White is a Los Angeles based artist who is represented by 1301 PE.

Selected Exhibitions & Reviews: 2007—*New Materials as New Media*, Contemporary Arts Center, Cincinnati, OH. *Vinyl*, Buenos Aires. *Los Angeles*, Spreuth Magers, Munich. Solo Exhibition, Hirshhorn Museum and Sculpture Garden, Washington, D.C. Solo Exhibition, China Art Objects Galleries, Los Angeles, CA. 2006—*Midnight*, Skestos Gabriele Gallery, Chicago, IL. Solo Exhibition, Sue Crockford Gallery, Auckland, New Zealand. Solo Exhibition, Paul Andriesse, Amsterdam. *La Triennale di Milano*, Milan. *Shanghai Biennale*, Shanghai. 2005—*Bazar*, Galerie Ghislaine Hussenot, Paris. *Periwinkles*, 1301 PE, Los Angeles, CA. Solo Exhibition, Hammer Museum, Los Angeles, CA. 2004—*Amps and Ohms*, centre d'art contemporain la Synagogue de Delme, Delme, France. *Past Present Future: Contemporary Art 1950-present*, The Art Institute of Chicago, Chicago, IL.

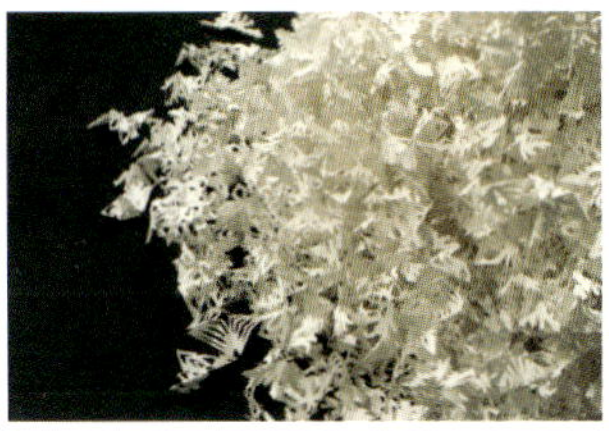

### WENDY WISCHER

*The desire to reflect on selected forms, objects and fragments, reveals how a single set of principles can be found all through the universe. Living in both rural and urban settings has brought two worlds together. The exposure to Ellen Dissanayake's Homoaestheticus created great interest in Earth Art, as the natural world stirs a nostalgic affection and strong sense of refined technology prove to be equally intoxicating. Galileo and his pursuit of truth and enlightenment depicted within the realms of poesy and innovation, have ignited a strong interest in the sciences and provided immeasurable inspiration. With a minimalist approach to form and reflection on process, I am lured the redefine the term environment, explore the impact of surrounding and include within them, the body exposed as landscape, the topography of technology embrace, time, space and memory mapped, and that which is difficult to utter, revealed.—WW*

Wendy Wischer maintains a studio in Miami, Florida, and is represented by David Castillo Gallery in Miami.

Selected Exhibitions & Awards. 2007—Pollock-Krasner Foundation Grant. *Artscapes*, Outdoor installtion, Cranden Nature Center, Key Biscayne, FL. 2006—*Fatamorgana*, Haifa Museum of Art, Haifa, Israel. *Night Air*, David Castillo Gallery, Miami, FL. *Transitory Patterns: Florida Women Artists*, National Museum of Women in the Arts, Washington, D.C. (touring to: Ft. Lauderdale Museum of Art, Ft. Lauderdale, FL; Deland Museum of Art, Deland, FL; Mary Brogan Museum of Art & Science, Tallahassee, FL). 2005—Individual Artist Fellowship, Florida Division of Cultural Affairs. *Marking Time*, Miami Art Museum, Miami FL. *Draw*, Son Espace, Girona, Spain. *Hope and Determination*, Alva Gallery, New London, CT. MACO, Diane Lowenstein Fine Arts, Mexico City. 2004—My Dream of You, Project Room at The Soap Factory, Minneapolis, MN. 2003—*Under the Spell of Maya*, Video projection, Design District, Miami, FL. *Full to Waiting and Back Again*, Out light projection, Miami Herald Building, Miami, FL. *Natural World*, Kimberly Venardos & Company, New York, NY. Alberta Prize for Visual Art, Alberta DuPont Bonsal Foundation. 2002—*to Remember*, site-specific installation, Project Room, Bernice Steinbaum Gallery, Miami, FL.

---

Pae White, *Noisy Letters (Blue)*, *Noisy Letters (Green)*, *Noisy Letters (Yellow)*, 2006, collage, 37 x 25 inches. Courtesy of the Artist and 1301PE, Los Angeles.

Wendy Wischer, Detail of *Longing*, 2004, cut paper, 18 x 16 inches diameter. Courtesy of the Artist and David Castillo Gallery, Miami.

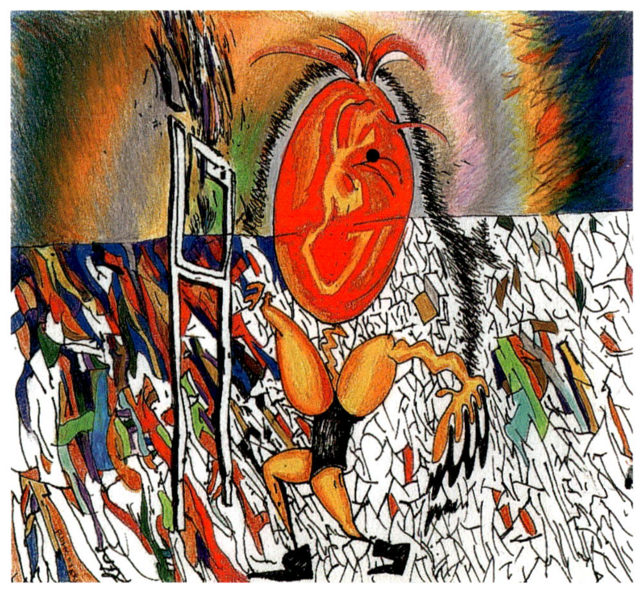

Above: Paul Rutkovsky, *Muscle Head*, 2005, pen and ink, colored pencil, 7 x 8 inches. Courtesy of the Artist.

### FLORIDA STATE UNIVERSITY

T. K. Wetherell, President

Lawrence G. Abele, Provost & VP for Academic Affairs

Sally McRorie, Dean, College of Visual Arts, Theatre & Dance

### MUSEUM STEERING COMMITTEE

Jack Freiberg, Assoc. Dean, CVAT&D

Richard K. Emmerson, Chair, Art History Department

Cameron Jackson, Director, School of Theatre

Lynn Hogan, Assoc. Dean, CVAT&D

Allys Palladino-Craig, Director, Museum of Fine Arts

Patty Phillips, Russell Sandifer, Co-Chairs, Dance Department

Marcia Rosal, Chair, Art Education Department

Joe Sanders, Chair, Art Department

Eric Wiedegreen, Chair Interior Design Department

### MUSEUM OF FINE ARTS STAFF

Allys Palladino-Craig, Director

Viki D. Thompson Wylder, Curator of Education

Jean D. Young, Collections Registrar / Fiscal Officer

Teri Yoo, Communications Officer

Wayne Vonada, Senior Preparator

Stephanie Tessin, Art in State Buildings / Special Projects

Events Staff: Lori Neuenfeldt and Stephanie Dutcher.
Interns: Michelle Newell, Editorial Assistant; Camille Davie.
Graduate Assistants: Becki Rutta and Seung Yeon Sang.

### VOLUNTEER COORDINATOR

Alyse Sedley

### ASSISTANTS

Kelly Paul
Ashley Hickman

### VOLUNTEERS

| | |
|---|---|
| Maxie Balthrop | Austen Kane |
| Margot Brody | Kara Leffler |
| Malcolm Craig | John Luthin |
| Katherine Farley | Rachel Thornton |
| Heidi Hargadon | Sara Turner |
| Ashley Jehle | Tom Wylder |